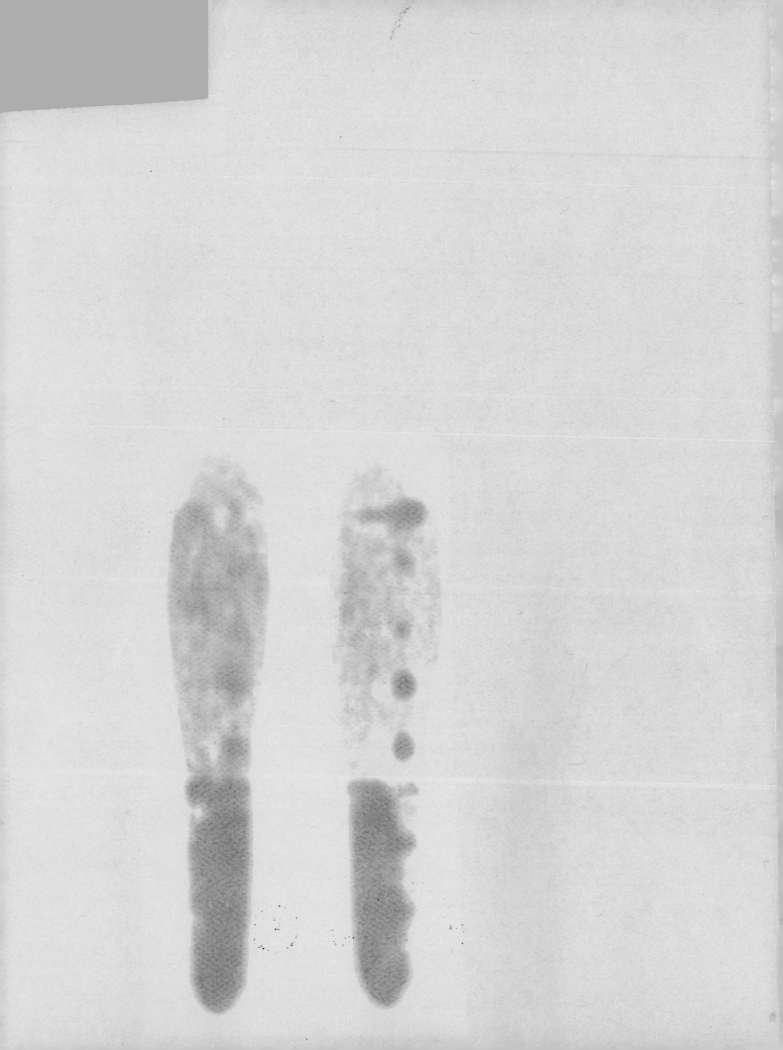

A
PATTERN
IDENTIFICATION
GUIDE

Gertrude Tatnall Jacobson

HAVILAND CHINA: VOLUME TWO

ISBN 0-87069-291-7
Library of Congress Catalog
Card No. 75-43372

Cover photograph: PAPILLON BLEU from the collection of Marie Kuhlman Gatshet.

Published by

Wallace-Homestead Book Co.
1912 Grand Avenue
Des Moines, Iowa 50305

Dedication

To

Opha Fightmaster, who taught me that the story of Haviland China had barely been tapped and with patience and kindness has kept me tapping and typing until I am as fascinated with the subject as she . . .

and to the late

Orville E. Kuhlman, whose unfailing gentle sense of humor started me on the way to becoming the photographic illustrator of this volume . . .

this book is affectionately dedicated.

Contents

Acknowledgments

It has always puzzled me that authors, when publishing a book, seemed to be indebted to so many people. I am not puzzled any more! Anyone spending almost two years researching and preparing a book for publication is physically incapable of working alone, sufficient unto himself. A book of this kind could not be written without other people for reasons of sheer logistics, if no other!

Publically expressing thanks to all who have contributed to this volume would be extremely difficult. Many of the contributors I have never met, nor even talked with on the telephone, and of this group, first and foremost go very real thanks to Monsieur Jean d'Albis, a direct descendant of the founder of the Haviland Company and historian of the Company. He lives in Limoges, France. Monsier d'Albis has been the essential keystone of the book's accuracy of detail and has been kind and cooperative far beyond the call of duty.

The cooperation of John H. Atkinson and his wife Laura, who live in Albuquerque, New Mexico, is a contribution of much appreciated note. Mr. Atkinson, too, is a lineal descendant of David Haviland, founder of the company, his mother having been Elsie Haviland, of Brooklyn, New York. During Mrs. Atkinson's lifetime, samples of Haviland sent to the New York salesroom seem to have gravitated her way, and through her son, John Atkinson, I had the pleasure of meeting some of her family in New Jersey, where I photographed many interesting examples. Mr. Edgar Hutto, husband of Mary Atkinson Hutto, is responsible for the greater part of the illustrations of the "eastern" Atkinson families' legacies of Haviland china, as my photography was frequently signally unsuccessful at that early stage.

The contributors of one, or of hundreds of patterns, include friends of long standing and also new friends whom I have met during the writing of this book. The two largest contributors of patterns, knowledge, and time are Orpha Fightmaster, one of the two people to whom this book is dedicated, and Marie Kuhlman Gatschet, whose late husband is the other. Mrs. Gatschet's extensive collection, as well as that of Mrs. Fightmaster, is only matched by the interest, time, and effort they have expended in helping to prepare this book for publication. To these two women, my most profound thanks! Following them are the contributors in alphabetical order, because each and every contribution is important, and the alphabet was devised, I am sure, so that a grateful author could express her appreciation impartially, bearing no personal responsibility for the spelling of last names.

The illustrations, particularly in black and white, except where otherwise noted, are predominately taken by me, under the painstaking tutelage of two wonderful commercial photographers who kept me afloat in a sea of problems due to inexperience. Roger F. Marshall and Walter E. Dickenman have made doubtful negatives into representative positives by careful developing and custom finishing; seasoning with praise when I was lucky, and curtain lectures when I thoroughly deserved them. Without these two men this book could not have been illustrated, particularly as a pattern guide.

Thanks to my secretary, Jean Gray — her help has been invaluable — and to Ann W. Hood, my friend and neighbor. My thanks for her forbearance through these long months when Haviland china has been an all-consuming interest, to the exclusion of the give and take of friendship.

Last, but not least, I am and will be eternally grateful to my husband, Alan Jacobson, who has been patience itself for all this time, with a constancy of good humor and encouragement upon which I have leaned with much gratitude.

To all these people, named and unnamed, my deepest gratitude and warmest affection.

— *Gerturde Tatnall Jacobson, A.S.A.*

Introduction to Volume Two

The Haviland Company, manufacturing dinnerware, was founded because of an incident in the lives of two Haviland brothers who ran a china store in New York City. In the course of their work they were asked to replace a broken piece of very fine French porcelain dinnerware and their inability to do so from their stock sent the younger brother, David, on a tour of France. After much searching the piece's origin was found near Limoges in central France.

This discovery was much appreciated by David Haviland who believed that a new source of supply had been unearthed. To his keen disappointment, however, the French manufacturer was not sufficiently flexible to change his methodology to conform to the wishes of the American buyer. The old adage "if you want a job done right, do it yourself" seemed to be the only solution to supplying the peculiar and particular American market with French porcelain that fitted American needs.

When he came to this decision he packed up his wife and young son and moved to Limoges, France, where be bought property and built a factory. His American heritage of independent thought and technical innovations ran afoul of French tradition, so that the first years posed many problems. The French way was to make the biscuit or greenware in Limoges and to ship it to Paris for decoration and glazing. This was too roundabout to suit David Haviland whose preference it was to design the blanks, turn out the greenware, decorate it, glaze it, and ship it to the United States — all, at least up to the shipping, from under one management and in one city. To do it his way he instituted an apprentice system with pupils and teachers of design in his factory at Limoges, and thus he broke the power of the long-entrenched French Guild system. This was not accomplished without strong objections (and even rioting) from the plentiful competition in Limoges. He seemed to thrive on difficulty, because each year his china production level rose like the tide, creating crushing competition for English china factories whose markets in the United States dwindled.

The Haviland story is a complex one. First it should be stressed that the Haviland family that ran the business from 1842 to 1973 were family members by direct descent from the founder. Not only was it a family business, but it was an American family business. No Haviland who managed the company ever allowed his American citizenship to lapse. The majority of the factory output throughout all those years was for the American trade. Even though it was made in France it was made *by* Americans *for* Americans. That was its primary object from the very beginning.

One of David Haviland's sons, Charles Edward Haviland, initiated an experimental station which was actually a research laboratory for the development of new and artistic approaches to the making of dinnerware. At Auteuil, near Paris, Charles started an atelier or workshop, and enlisted some of the well-known Impressionists to try their hands at expressing artistic ideas in ceramics. A group of chapters in *Volume One* is devoted to the experimental works of art produced at the Auteuil atelier. These works, were expressed in bisque statuary, porcelain, stoneware, and particularly in terra-cotta vases and jardinieres. The examples that are still extant are fascinating.

Volume Two is devoted to the unraveling of the mysteries associated with identifying Haviland dinnerware. Thousands upon thousands of patterns were designed and made for sale in the United States, but only about 725 of these patterns had a name by which to call themselves. Identifying and naming patterns and color coding them so that can be matched with patterns belonging to readers is what these books are basically about. Naturally, the identification job will not be completed in these two volumes, but future supplements to these volumes will strive toward this ultimate goal. The supplements will be published when sufficient unknown patterns are presented to the author on loan, giving her the opportunity to make an identification, afix a name by which the pattern can be known, and to take one more "unknown" out of circulation.

List of Contributors

Inevitably in an identification guide of this type there were duplications of patterns, and priority had to be given to those examples that were first received. We are grateful and deeply appreciative of the interest shown by all of our contributors and regret that all contributions could not be published. If you have contributed a distinct pattern which inadvertently has not been published, please accept our apologies and resubmit it for a future supplement. *G.T.J.*

Number	Name	Location
1	Fightmaster, Orpha	Platte City, Mo.
2	Gatschet, Marie Kuhlman	Kansas City, Mo.
3	Alden, Aimée Neff	Memphis, Tenn.
4	Arnold, Mrs. James H.	Denver, Colo.
5	Atkinson, Mr. & Mrs. Edward Haviland	State College, Pa.
6	Atkinson, Mr. & Mrs. F. W.	Medford, N.J.
7	Atkinson, Mr. & Mrs. John H.	Albuquerque, N.M.
8	Ault, Vern E.	Independence, Mo.
9	Bachman, the late Mrs. William S.	Southport, Conn.
10	Barnes, Major and Mrs. W. J.	Albuquerque, N.M.
11	Barwin, Frances M.	Albuquerque, N.M.
12	Bell, Ernestine R.	Ocala, Fla.
13	Benjamin, Mr. & Mrs. James W.	Kansas City, Mo.
14	Bisbee, Wallace A.	Albuquerque, N.M.
15	Brock, Mrs. B. E.	Middletown, Ohio
16	Brown, Mrs. J. M.	Albuquerque, N.M.
17	Canon, Virginia	Findlay, Ill.
18	Chapman, June A.	Memphis, Tenn.
19	Cillissen, Mrs. George	Corrales, N.M.
20	Claassen, Evelyn Strong	Phoenix, Ariz.
21	Colby, Mrs. Gordon	Woodbridge, Conn.
22	Conners, Mrs. Robert	Crete, Nebraska
23	Cooper, Mrs. Hugh P.	Albuquerque, N.M.
24	Cornelison, Mrs. Woodrow	Tijeras, N.M.
25	Crouch, Kay Hall (Mrs. Robert)	Scottsdale, Ariz.
26	d'Albis, Monsieur Jean	Limoges, France
27	Dixon, Mrs. Lawrence	Corrales, N.M.
28	Fenger, Jan	Old Saybrook, Conn.
29	Fullerton, Irene	Albuquerque, N.M.
30	Grammer, M.	Albuquerque, N.M.
31	Gray, Cortenia F.	Colorado Springs, Colo.
32	Gray, Jean I.	Albuquerque, N.M.
33	Gray, Lucille H.	Albuquerque, N.M.
34	Griswold, Mrs. Gilbert	Albuquerque, N.M.
35	Hamm, Larry W.	Middletown, Ohio
36	Harlacher, Mrs. Lloyd	Albuquerque, N.M.
37	Helt, Gladys R.	Durhamville, N.Y.
38	Hepner, Paul E., Jr.	Albuquerque, N.M.
39	Hickox, Mrs. Richard T.	Albuquerque, N.M.
40	Hite, Barbara W.	Anchorage, Ky.
41	Hollingworth, Mrs. W. D.	Albuquerque, N.M.
42	Horvitz, Mrs. Sam (via Ralph and Terry Kovel)	Shaker Heights, Ohio

Number	Name	Location
43	Howard, Mrs. Harry Buckner	Albuquerque, N.M.
44	Huff, Clarence	Bernalillo, N.M.
45	Hurley, Milas L.	Albuquerque, N.M.
46	Hutto, Mr. & Mrs. Edgar, Jr.	Cherry Hill, N.J.
47	Hynes, Yvonne K.	Vestal, N.Y.
48	Jacobson, Dr. & Mrs. Alan	Albuquerque, N.M.
49	Kalin, Mrs. Jay	Kansas City, Mo.
50	Kirk, Mrs. Carter	Deming, N.M.
51	Lampman, Mr. & Mrs. William W.	Santa Fe, N.M.
52	Larsen Wager, Mrs. Janet	Albuquerque, N.M.
53	Lewis, Mrs. Frank M.	Albuquerque, N.M.
54	Lindeman, Sue E.	Indianapolis, Ind.
55	Louthan, the late Mrs. Earl	Albuquerque, N.M.
56	McDonagh, Virginia R.	Canton, Ohio
57	McEwen, Mrs. Willard Lewis	West Chester, Pa.
58	Morgans, the late Helen Ree	Albuquerque, N.M.
59	Motto, Sytha	Albuquerque, N.M.
60	Murphy, Mr. & Mrs. Emmett	Albuquerque, N.M.
61	Neiswander, Kenneth C.	Albuquerque, N.M.
62	Pierce, Grace B.	Albuquerque, N.M.
63	Pope, Mrs. Alan	Albuquerque, N.M.
64	Price, George	Kansas City, Mo.
65	Robertson, Mr. & Mrs. Jack B.	Kansas City, Mo.
66	Rogers, Mrs. James W.	Albuquerque, N.M.
67	Romanet, Celeste	Limoges, France
68	Rugen, Mrs. Catherine E.	Chicago, Ill.
69	Schreiver, Charles	Albuquerque, N.M.
70	Schuster, Mrs. Shirl J.	St. Louis, Mo.
71	Smith, Mrs. A. C., Jr.	Kansas City, Mo.
72	Smith, Diana	Garden Grove, Calif.
73	Spake, Elizabeth Hird	Leesburg, Va.
74	Spake, Robert H.	Leesburg, Va.
75	Stevens, Betty	Albuquerque, N.M.
76	Strong, Mrs. George T.	Albuquerque, N.M.
77	Tod, Mrs. David B.	Santa Fe, N.M.
78	Torrens, Dr. & Mrs. John K.	Albuquerque, N.M.
79	Ussery, Mrs. T. Albert	Albuquerque, N.M.
80	Vytlacil, Mrs. Nicholas	Albuquerque, N.M.
81	Walker, Lee & Marge	Athens, Ohio
82	Weaver, Halene M. (Mrs. C. R.)	Albuquerque, N.M.
83	White, Mrs. Clayton S.	Nicholls Hills, Okla.
84	White, Eileen D.	Albuquerque, N.M.
85	Whitlow, W. C.	Fulton, Mo.
86	Wilcox, Josephine M.	Albuquerque, N.M.
87	Wilson, Marguerite W.	Salinas, Calif.
88	Wood, the late Mrs. Morris W.	West Chester, Pa.
89	Woodell, Mrs. Tessie K.	Albuquerque, N.M.
90	Zickefoose, Marian	Elmhurst, Ill.
91	Musée Adrien Dubouche	Limoges France

Author's Note

Names for patterns and blanks come from three sources. The factory-named pieces are identified with one asterisk, and common usage has dictated the names of pieces marked with double asterisks. The third and largest category goes unmarked: the names are the arbitrary selections of the author who feels that Haviland owners like to have a name by which to call their pattern.

It is hoped that the identification system will be simpler to use, as well as easier to remember, because of this arbitrary decision.

I Identifying Your Haviland Pattern

The first step in the process of identification is recognizing the backmark. The backmark proves conclusively that the pattern was made by the Haviland Company at some stage in its history. There is a certain chronology clearly defined in the company annals, but there is overlapping, and there are other differences which can be readily explained in the light of the mechanical slips that they were. The earliest mark was incised or cut into the paste before the glaze was applied and fired, or was embossed at the same stage. These various backmarks, starting with the two just mentioned will be charted and numbered, with dates, wherever possible. The mark *Haviland and Company* is in green, and is under the glaze; this is the factory mark. Another mark is usually present, and that mark is over the glaze and in a contrasting color. This is the decorator's mark. This is of less concern to us than the factory mark, so it is with only the factory mark that we shall deal. The system that we are inaugurating here is *alphabetical* to identify backmarks in accordance with the chart, and *names* to identify patterns. Pattern names will be numbered by the number of the illustration as it appears. All patterns illustrated in this book may be located by name in the alphabetical index.

There are three categories of pattern names: (1) factory-chosen names, identified with one asterisk; (2) pattern names acquired from common usage, identified with two asterisks; (3) pattern names that are the selections of the author, bearing no asterisks. This last category is the largest. It is the author's strong opinion, as mentioned in the "Author's Note" preceding this chapter, that the American people like to know the *name* by which to speak of their possessions. A name is much more of a clue to identity than is a number, paticularly in the depersonalizing times in which we are living. We are identified by our Social Security numbers, our bank account numbers, our charge account and credit card numbers, our automobile registrations, our hospital and doctor's records, and by probably many more computer banks than we are even aware. As mentioned elsewhere in this book, Mrs. Arlene Schleiger has identified over 1,000 patterns using, of course, the names placed on a pattern at the factory, but otherwise using numbers plus the alphabet to differentiate between a given pattern on one blank from the same pattern on any number of other blanks. These patterns, so identified, are only a small proportion of the total Haviland output. In these books many patterns here identified by name have never previously been identified.

The backmark gives a clue as to the chronological identification of a pattern, because if it is marked in any of the varieties of Haviland and Company backmarks available you will know better than to look for the blank among those produced by Theodore Haviland, and vice versa. The chart will help you to recognize backmarks with rapidity.

(continued on page 160)

Haviland Backmarks

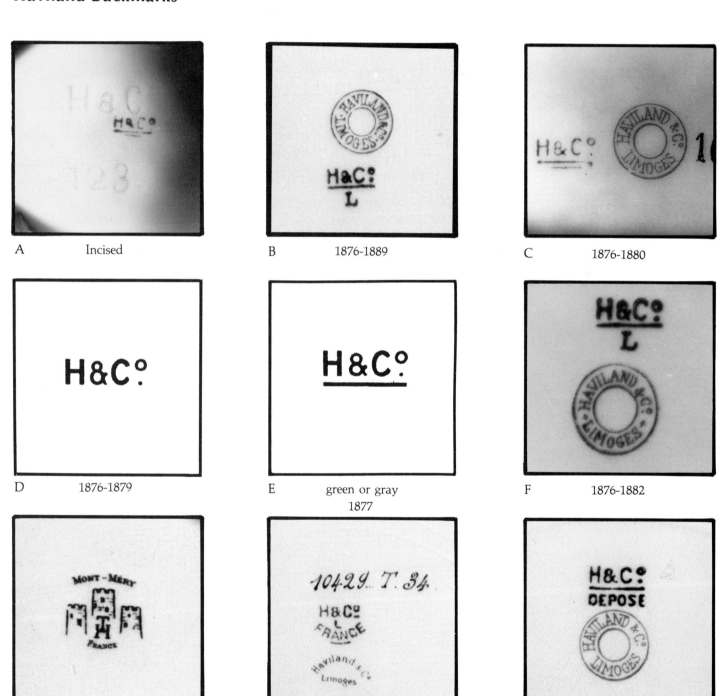

A   Incised

B   1876-1889

C   1876-1880

D   1876-1879

E   green or gray
1877

F   1876-1882

G   1892

H   1893-1896

I   1887

J   1893

K

L   Incised

M

N   1894

O   1894

P   1895

Q   1895

R   1903

S   1903

T   1925

U   1920-1936

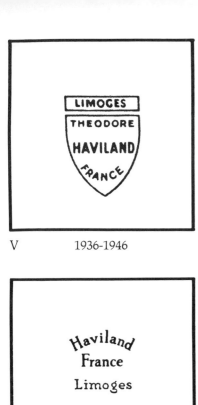

V   1936-1946

W   Incised in the paste.
1894-1957

X   1962

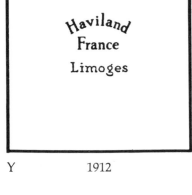

Y   1912

Z

AA

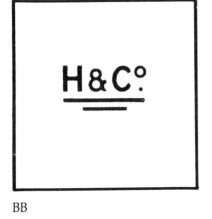

BB

CC

DD   Incised in paste.

MADE IN FRANCE
BY FRANK HAVILAND
PARIS - AUTEUIL

DÉCOR DÉPOSÉ - REGISTERED

EE

FF

H&C°

GG

HH   Door Bolt in low relief.

II

JJ

KK

LL

MM

NN

OO

PP

QQ   1878-1883

RR

SS

TT

UU   Reduced Auteuil

VV   Auteuil

WW

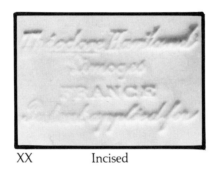

XX   Incised

The next step is determining the blank, remembering that when you look for a matching blank to fit the backmark it is the beginning of a successful search. A blank is the form that an article would have if it had no decoration upon it, which is why all pieces which are all white and without any colored decoration have no names. When a piece is trimmed with gold alone, it also assumes the nameless state. In the rare instances where the company annals do not provide a definite name for a blank the author has again arbitrarily assigned a blank name. The time may come when I shall have to print a retraction for an arbitrarily named blank, but I should be pleased to do so if new information should appear that puts me in the wrong. Also, the arbitrary naming of the very rare blank not factory-named means one less number to have to keep straight, and one less mystery to solve!

The next step will concern itself with patterns, and it is to be remembered that *it is patterns that are named.* Any pattern can be substantially changed in appearance on each different blank, and this sometimes makes it difficult to decide whether the pattern is really the same in all cases. This is why the pattern section in Volume Two uses, wherever possible, a plate or saucer, as the surface is comparatively flat; hence the pattern can be relatively uniform from one piece to another. This should make it easier to discover *your* pattern, whatever its blank.

The photographs of patterns are numbered in sequence, *named* from whatever source, and are further identified by the size of the illustrated piece, the blank it appears on, the backmark on the back, and whether it is a product of Haviland and Company or Theodore Haviland Company. Following the company designation is a number in parentheses which represents the name of the contributor. Names and numbers of the many contributors of Haviland patterns may be found on page 10.

Should you not be able to find your own pattern among those illustrated, do not either be surprised nor distressed, as there were thousands of patterns produced, and not all of them could possibly appear in two volumes. These books are intended to be a kind of "teaser" to stimulate Haviland collectors into wanting to have patterns named and identified. They were written, in fact, to start the clearing up of 20,000 mysteries!

Haviland and Co. Blanks

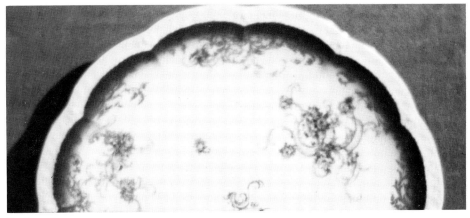

Bowknots*

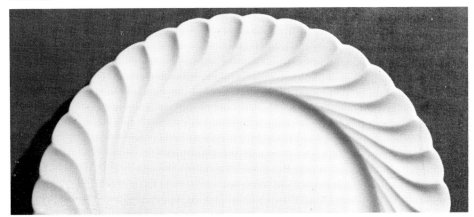

Cannelé

Cannelé, Straight*

Club du Barry

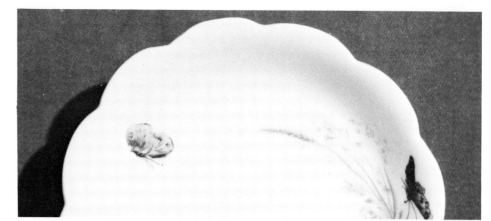

Crescent

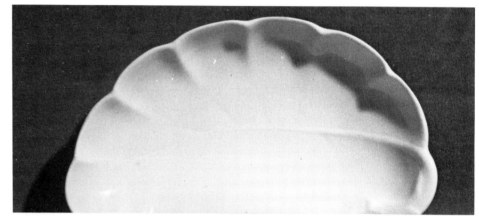

Crescent Leaf

Crows'foot

Diamond

Diana

Double Scallops*

Embroidery*

Eyelet*

Fiddle*

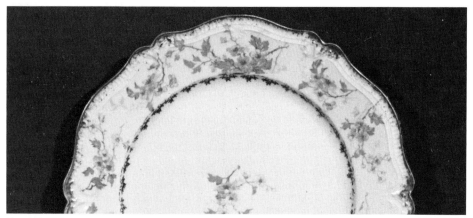

Fluted Ruffle*

Gabrielle*

Henri II

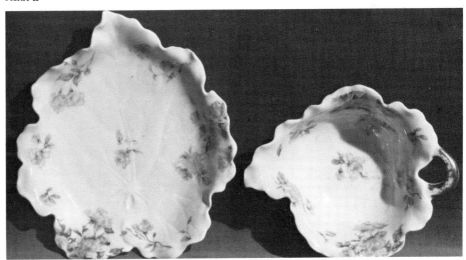

Leaf

Marseille

165

Napkin Fold or Oxford

Nenuphar

Nenuphar, Plain*

166

Ormolu Buckles*

Osier (one of several)

Osier (one of several)

Palme

167

Papillon

Plain

Pompadour

Pompadour II

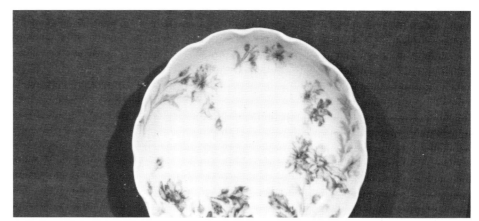

Portia

President

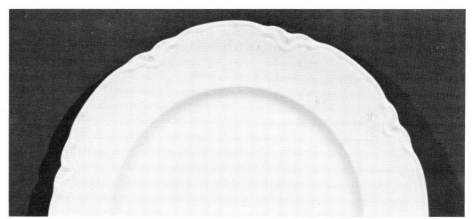

Ranson

Saxon

Saxon-on-Claws

Seed Pearls*

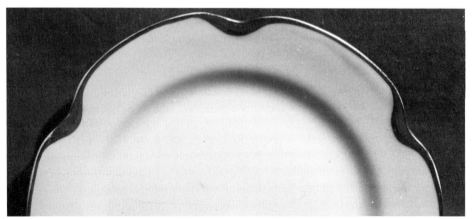

Silver

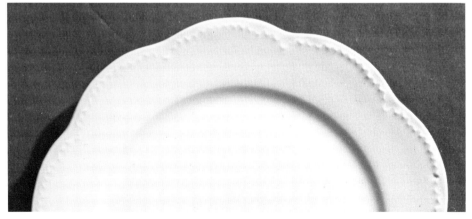

Star

Strasburg

Tutu*

Vermicelle*

Yedo

171

Theodore Haviland Blanks

Aigle

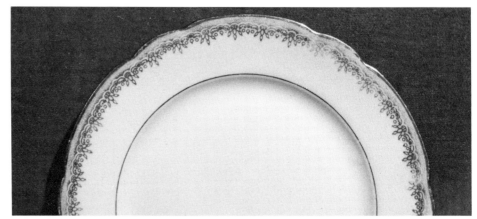

Alternate Scallops*

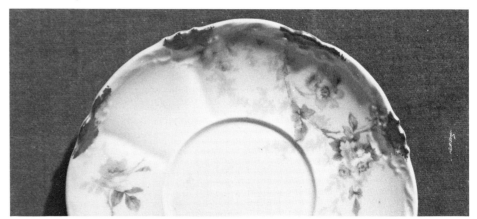

Caroline

Chippendale

Diamond

Embossed*, St. Cloud

Fantaisie

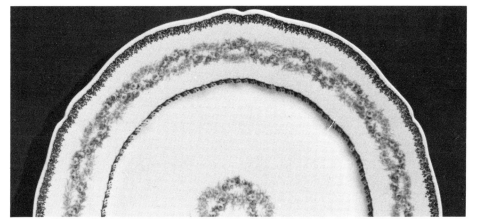

Feston-Chêne

173

Geisha

Juliet

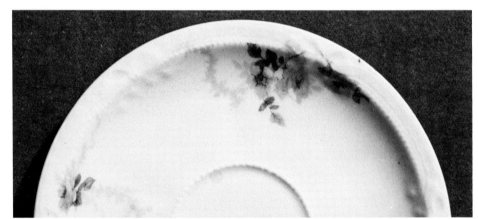

Lambelle

Louis XV

174

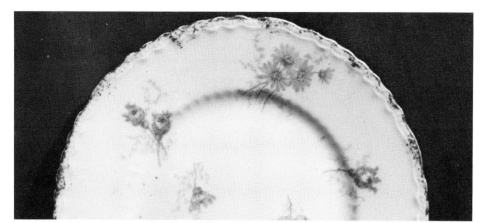

Marie Antoinette

Parabère

Pilgrim

Plain

175

Pompadour

Romeo

Rouen

Ruby

176

St. Cloud

St. Germain

St. Raphael

Swanson*

177

Theo Ranson

Triple Ripple*

Wavelets*

**American
Theodore Haviland Blank**

Wheat

178

To implement this, supplements will be published as quickly and as often as those people who cannot locate their patterns in these volumes send the author a plate for identification, and enough such patterns accumulate to fill a supplement. Hopefully, supplements will continue to be published until at least the majority of the mysteries are solved. To achieve this goal, *you*, the reader, are both basically involved and personally responsible. The method is simple. Prior to sending off a package of mysterious patterns, drop me a line saying that the patterns are on the way and by what carrier they are coming. Pack each piece separately, using no less than four thicknesses of newspaper, and then packing them all, if more than one, in a strong cardboard carton. Next, pack that box firmly into a larger cardboard carton, insulating the inner box from damage by plenty of crumpled newspaper. Nothing should be allowed to shift within either box. Then insure and ship. All examples sent are loans, not donations, and the burden of expense is on me except for the shipping charges *to* me; so when you send me samples, insurance for their safe arrival is essential.

While under my roof your mysteries will be covered by my insurance. They will be photographed, cataloged, researched, named, and color-coded before being returned to you by insured carrier. Don't be worried if this takes quite a long time. They are safe while in my care, but remember that all of the work that has to be done on each piece takes time, with particular emphasis on photography. Assembling thirty-six pieces of china to use up a roll of film is in itself time-consuming, and it would be foolhardy on my part to return your china before the finished photograph is in my hands and proves to be photographically pressworthy. Unless it is a good, clear photograph, it is very difficult to reproduce it a second time in print and still have an identifiable pattern.

The recording procedure has been developed by trial and error and has proved accurate and uniform. The same meticulous records will be kept of all examples of patterns sent me for supplements as was done when compiling these books. Credits for contributions to supplements will be handled as they are in this volume.

Color coding is the final important task to be worked out in the identification of your Haviland. Accompanying this book is a removable color chart which groups colors into color families. There are seventy different colors, and with the exception of a true cobalt blue, a royal purple, and an eggplant shade called "aubergine," any colors you encounter in Haviland china will be represented either exactly or in tints lighter or shades darker than one of the color chips. These are, as you see, numbered, and it is by those numbers that you can code the colors on your china. It requires a good strong light, preferably daylight, to color-code well, but you will be surprised at how soon you will be able, with a degree of flexibility that is necessary to compensate for human differences in color sense, to take any piece of Haviland photographed in black-and-white and see it in your mind's eye in living color.

Look forward in the book to the examples of color coding beneath a photograph, follow the reference to the color chart, and the system will make sense. In fact, look for *your* pattern! If you find it, great, but if your colors are from different families entirely, and I have not mentioned this new family, please ship me a saucer (they are usually in long supply as cups are more fragile) and I will put the variation into the next supplement, with credit to you as contributor. Incidentally, if a color number appears often in large flowers and small and is repeated for buds and on foliage too, it will be only mentioned once under each heading listed.

You see it is not only new patterns I want to identify, it is new color differences in already named patterns as well. This method is necessary for maintaining accuracy and consistency to the detective work involved in the solving of 20,000 mysteries. I wish you good luck in your search, much pleasure and satisfaction, and offer the opportunity for you, the reader, to enlarge the knowledge of Haviland china for collectors everywhere.

Haviland and Co. Patterns

273. CHESTNUT HILL plate, 9⁵/₈″ diameter. Blank: *Seed Pearls**.
Backmark: J. Color code: Conventional border, three shades darker
than 22 plus gold. H & Co. (7).

274. STRATFORD-ON-AVON tea and toast tray, 8³/₈″ long. Blank:
Unknown. Backmark: H. Color code: Flowers, 5 touched with white.
Foliage, 70. Ribbon, 56, 63. H & Co. (1).

275. STURBRIDGE oyster plate, 8¾″ diameter. Blank: *Unknown.* Backmark: J. Color code: Border, 2, gold. Flowers, shades of 2 touched with 42; white. Small flowers, 64, 65 touched with 2; shades of 2 touched with white and two shades darker than 21; 42 touched with 2. Two shades darker than 21 touched with 2 and 6. Foliage, 18, 19, 20, 21 touched with 2, 42. H & Co. (1).

276. WINDBLOWN relish dish, 4½″ x 5½″. Blank: *Ranson.* Backmark: J. Color code: Flowers, 5, 6. Foliage, 28, 29, 30. H & Co. (58).

277. LA FETE saucer, 5³⁄₈″ diameter. Blank: *Plain.* Backmark: J. Color code: Border, 45. Background, light cream. Flowers, 60, two shades lighter than 45; two shades lighter than 13. Foliage, 21, 65. Cavetto, white with floral medallion. H & Co. (15).

278. ROTHENBURG plate, 8½″ diameter. Blank: *Diana.* Backmark: J. Color code: Foliage one and two shades lighter than 40 shading to 67 outlined in 6. Flowers, 50, 5 fading to white, two shades darker than 6, three shades lighter than 2. H & Co. (1).

279. LAURIE* saucer, 5¾" diameter. Blank: *Plain.* Backmark: RR. Color code: Band, 13 and gold. Amer. Theo. (1).

280. ROPER plate, 9¾" diameter. Blank: *Plain.* Backmark: J. Color code: Conventional border in 29, 30, outlined in 13. H & Co. (52).

281. ARLINGTON* demitasse saucer, 5" diameter. Blank: *Plain.* Backmark: RR. Color code: Flowers, 6 touched and outlined in 2; 2 touched with 60, 42; 42 touched with 2; 60 touched with 42 and 2. Foliage, 21 outlined in 2. Amer. Theo. (1).

282. ROXANNE saucedish, 5⅛" diameter. Blank: *Plain.* Backmark: D. Color code: Flowers and foliage, 43, 45, 42, 34, 60, one shade lighter than 40, 15. H & Co. (15).

283. PARKLAND plate, 8½" diameter. Blank: *Crow'sfoot.* Backmark: J. Color code: Border two shades lighter than 37. Flowers, 3, 4. Foliage, 20, 21, 22. Tiny leaves, 26. H & Co. (7).

285. WISCONSIN coupe-shaped plate, 7½" diameter. Blank: *Ranson.* Backmark: J. Color code: Flowers, 4, two shades darker than 4; 32, 34. Foliage, 22, three shades lighter than 22 touched with two shades darker than 4. H & Co. (12).

284. UNNAMED plate, 8½" diameter. Blank: *Diana.* Backmark: H. Color code: Band of 8 with gold. H & Co. (6).

286. ROSAMOND cup and saucer. Cup, 3⅛" diameter, 2" tall. Saucer, 5¼". Blank: *Diana.* Backmark: H. Color code: Flowers, 3, 42. Foliage, 68. Background ten shades lighter than 49 shading to cream. H & Co. (6).

184

287. UNNAMED cup and saucer. Saucer, 5³⁄₈". Blank: *Plain.*
Backmark: J. Color code: Gold border, chased. H & Co. (2).

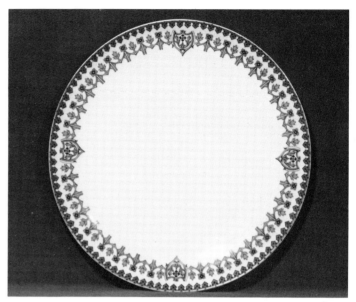

288. ROSEMARY coupe-shaped dessert plate, 7½" diameter. Blank:
Plain. Backmark: J. Color code: Conventional border with flowers
two shades darker than 5 and black. Leaves, 42 and black. H & Co.
(17).

289. ANDROMACHE plate, 9½" diameter. Blank: *Diana.*
Backmark: H. Color code: Background, 61. Ribbon, 20, two shades
lighter than 22. Other decoration, gold. H & Co. (2).

290. HERB OF GRACE cup and saucer. Cup, 3¼" in diameter, 2¹⁄₈"
tall. Saucer, 5¼". Blank: *Diana.* Backmark: B. Color code:
Flowers, 48 touched with 2, 65. Foliage, 30, four shades lighter than 30.
H & Co. (6).

291. HARVEST GLORY pitcher, 5½" tall. Blank: *Anchor.* Backmark: B plus impressed English Registry mark and ½ pint. Color code: Background, white with 4¼" border of 10. Handle, rope and anchor outlined in gold. Flowers, four shades lighter than 2; 3, white, 65, 66. Foliage, 38, 40, 13. Buds, 13. H & Co. (2).

293. HADDAM open vegetable bowl, 10" by 6⁵/₁₆" by 3¼". Blank: *Crescent.* Backmark: B. Color code: Flowers, 56, two shades lighter than 15, 29. Foliage, 22, 56, 29. H & Co. (46).

292. HIDALGO saucer, 5³/₈" diameter. Blank: *Plain.* Backmark: J. Color code: Conventional border, two shades lighter than 29, two shades darker than 47. Flowers, 4, 3, white. Foliage, 25. H & Co. (12).

294. HUNT plate, 8⁵/₈" diameter. Blank: *Plain.* Backmark: J. Color code: Flowers, 13; centers, 29. Foliage, one shade lighter than 29 outlined in 13. H & Co. (1).

295. UNNAMED plate, 8⁵/₈″ diameter. Blank: *Ranson.* Backmark: H. Color code: Band, two shades lighter than 2. H & Co. (6).

296. EVERGREEN VALLEY demitasse cup and saucer. Saucer, 4¾″ diameter. Blank: *Osier.* Backmark: E. Color code: Flowers, 61, 62, 2, 42, 56, 53. Foliage, 22, 20, 53, 68. H & Co. (2).

297. SLEEPY HOLLOW cup and saucer. Saucer, 4⁵/₁₆″ diameter. Blank: *Plain.* Backmark: B. Color code: Flowers, 24, 25 outlined in 13. Spotted foliage two shades lighter than 29. Shadows one shade darker than 18. H & Co. (20).

298. LUCINDA saucer, 5½″ diameter. Blank: *Plain.* Backmark: J. Color code: Flowers, 1 touched with 2, 67. Foliage, 28 touched with 59. H & Co. (15).

299. CHRYSANTHEMUM** plate, 9¾" diameter. Blank: *Marseille.* Backmark: J. Color code: Flowers and foliage, 50, 61, 8, 58, white, 24, 68, 70 touched with shades of 14. H & Co. (52).

300. MAYO saucer, 5⅜" diameter. Blank: *Star.* Backmark: J. Color code: Flowers, 42, 6, touched with three shades lighter than 14. Foliage, 28, 18. H & Co. (56).

301. AUTUMN NASTURTIUMS plate, 7½" diameter. Blank: *Diana.* Backmark: B. Color code: Flowers, 13, two shades darker than 13, 48, two shades darker than 30. H & Co. (6).

302. BLESSING WAY saucer, 5⅞" diameter. Blank: *Plain.* Backmark: B. Color code: Flowers and foliage two shades darker than 70; 49 touched with 10. Grasses two shades lighter than 61. H & Co. (28).

303. COUNTY CLARE saucer, 5³/₈" diameter. Blank: *Silver.* Backmark: J. Color code: Foliage and flowers, 33, 22, 3. H & Co. (15).

304. SUZETTE plate, 6¹/₈" diameter. Blank: *Ranson.* Backmark: J. Color code: Flowers, 5, 4, 3 with touches of 2. Foliage, 29 touched with 64 and 2. Shadows, 23, 24. H & Co. (3).

305. LAGUAYRA saucer, 5³/₈" diameter. Blank: *Plain.* Backmark: J. Color code: Flowers, 4 touched with 2. Foliage, 27, one shade lighter than 28. H & Co. (15).

306. VALKYRIE plate, 7¼" diameter. Blank: *Plain.* Backmark: B. Color code: Flowers, 47, 42, two shades lighter than 36, two shades darker than 6; 1, 41, 2, five shades lighter than 2; 9. Foliage three shades darker than 31; 22, 27 outlined in 49. H & Co. (12).

307. WINTERHAVEN saucer, 5³/₈" diameter. Blank: *Plain*. Backmark: J. Color code: Conventional border on cream. Flowers two shades lighter than 57, two shades darker than 42. Floral scrolls two shades lighter than 57, touched with 47. H & Co. (15).

308. TELLURIDE dinner plate, 9½" diameter. Blank: *Plain*. Backmark: J. Color code: Flowers, 42, 5, 13. Foliage, 29, 28, 27, 25. H & Co. (17).

309. SHALLCROSS plate, 6¹/₈" diameter. Blank: *Gabrielle**. Backmark: J. Color code: Flowers, 2, 42, 3, white. Foliage, 29 touched with 2. H & Co. (40).

310. RADNOR cup and saucer. Saucer, 5½" diameter. Blank: *Strasburg*. Backmark: H. Color code: Flowers, 56, 63 touched with two shades lighter than 2, white. Foliage, 59, 69. H & Co. (56).

311. PRINCESS* plate, 8½" diameter. Blank: *Star.* Backmark: J. Color code: Flowers, 1, white. Foliage, 27. Stems, 40. Scrolls, 36. Note: This Princess pattern is the standard pattern although more scattered than the prototype. H & Co. (78).

312. OLD SAYBROOK saucer, 5³⁄₈" diameter. Blank: *Plain.* Backmark: J. Color code: Flowers, 1, two shades lighter than 2, 42. Foliage, 21 touched with 42, 2. H & Co. (28).

313. NASHA cup and saucer. Saucer, 4¾" diameter. Blank: *Silver.* Backmark: J. Color code: Flowers, 5, 6 touched with 4. Foliage, 19, 18. H & Co. (56).

314. MASTERSON beanery, 5⁷⁄₈". Blank: *Star.* Backmark: J. Color code: Flowers, 42, 64, 65, 6, 5. Foliage, 29, four shades darker than 69, 30. H & Co. (38).

315. LARKIN luncheon plate, 8½″ diameter. Blank: *Marseille.*
Backmark: H. Color code: Flowers and foliage, 35, 28, outlined in
two shades lighter than 15. H & Co. (47).

316. JOHANNESBERG dinner plate, 9¾″ diameter. Blank: *Plain.*
Backmark: J. Color code: Conventional border, 63, 12, 28. H & Co.
(17).

317. HITCHCOCK vegetable bowl, 9½″ wide by 3½″ tall. Blank:
Plain. Backmark: J. Color code: Flowers, 1, 11, 52, 54. Foliage, 21,
34. H & Co. (46).

318. GAYLE leaf fruit dish (salesman's sample). 5″ by 5¼″. Blank:
Leaf. Backmark: B, factory #4758, Feuille K. Color code: Flowers,
59, 60, 61, 62, 42, 65. Foliage, 36. H & Co. (1).

319. FLOWERING FRUIT TREE saucer, 5⁷/₈″ diameter. Blank: *Star.*
Backmark: B. Color code: Flowers, 3, 4, white. Foliage, 29, white
touched with 4. Shadows, 67. H & Co. (78).

321. DALHOUSIE bowl, 9¼″ diameter. Blank: *Star.* Backmark: J.
Color code: Flowers, 5, 11, 65, 66, touches of 13 with gold. Foliage, 20,
21. H & Co. (71).

320. ESTANCIA saucer, 5³/₈″ diameter. Blank: *Plain.* Backmark: J.
Color code: Conventional border, 6, 32, one shade darker than 41.
Flowers, 6. Foliage, three shades lighter than 29, 25. H & Co. (12).

322. CARLOTTA saucer, 5¼″ diameter. Blank: *Bowknots**. Backmark: J. Color code: Flowers, 3, 4. Foliage, 26, 27. H & Co. (47).

323. BREWSTER plate, 6¼" diameter. Blank: *Star.* Backmark: J.
Color code: Flowers, 3, 4, white. Foliage, 27 touched with 4. H & Co.
(81).

324. ANCESTRY plate, 7¼" diameter. Blank: *Plain.* Backmark: B.
Color code: Foliage and berries, 15, 69, 70; berries touched with
enamel. H & Co. (65).

325. ANDANTE plate, 10³/₈" diameter. Blank: *Plain.* Backmark: J.
Color code: Foliage two shades lighter than 29. Border three shades
lighter than 13, 49. Central border one shade lighter than 36, 16, 25. H
& Co. (13).

326. AMBER fruit dish, 5" diameter. Blank: *Plain.* Backmark: J.
Color code: Conventional border, 45 touched with 13. H & Co. (7).

327. ROSALINDE* bread and butter plate, 6½" diameter. Blank: *Pilgrim.* Backmark: RR. Color code: Flowers, 69 with white touched in 16, shades of 5; 6 touched in 69, white, 16. Two shades darker than 60, 60 touched with white, 16. Foliage, 21 touched with 16 and 5 with 69. Shadow, 6. Amer. Theo. (1).

328. CASTLE COMBE domed butter server with insert, 8" over handles. Blank: *Portia.* Backmark: J. Color code: Flowers, 54, 56, two shades lighter than 6, white, two shades lighter than 42. Foliage, 26, 63. H & Co. (79).

329. SOPHISTICATE sugar bowl, 7¼" to tip of finial. Blank: *Ruby.* Backmark: A. Color code: Bands, 8 outlined black; trim on handles and finial black. H & Co. (1).

330. SCHERZO saucer, 5½" diameter. Blank: *Plain.* Backmark: J. Color code: Flowers, 4, 5, 7, 58. Folige, 29, two and four shades lighter than 29. Stems, 12. Shadows one shade lighter than 58. H & Co. (78).

331. MAZURKA cup and saucer. Saucer, 4¼″ diameter. Blank: *Diana.* Backmark: I. Color code: Flowers, 64, 25. Foliage, 25, 15. Berries, 64. H & Co. (2).

332. SHIRLEY fruit dish, 5″ diameter. Blank: *Star.* Backmark: J. Color code: Flowers, 1, 4, three shades lighter than 2, four shades lighter than 53. Foliage, 28, 27. H & Co. (56).

333. BOYDEN demitasse cup, 2⅛″ tall by 2⅛″ in diameter. Blank: *Plain.* Backmark: J. Color code: Conventional border, 42, 69, black. H & Co. (28).

334. JOCELYN plate, 9⅝″ diameter. Blank: *Diana.* Backmark: B. Color code: Flowers, 64 fading to white, 70 outlined in 13. Foliage, two shades lighter than 28, 69. H & Co. (7).

335. SERENITY butter pat, 3½″ diameter. Blank: *Diana.* Backmark: A. Color code. Flowers, 4, 45, 2. Foliage, 29, 33, 28. H & Co. (62).

336. MARIKA plate, 8⅜″ diameter. Blank: *Star.* Backmark: J. Color code: Border, three shades lighter than 36, 20. Flowers, one shade darker than 1. Foliage, 29. H & Co. (58).

337. LE PAYSAGE plate, 6⅛″ diameter. Blank: *Ranson.* Backmark: J. Color code: Flowers, 3 touched with 4. Foliage, 26 touched with three shades lighter than 13. Shadows, 68. H & Co. (12).

338. SERENA coupe-shaped plate, 7½″ diameter. Blank: *Gabrielle*.* Backmark: J. Color code: Flowers, 61, to white touched with 20. Foliage, 20 touched with 4. Shadows, 67. H & Co. (1).

197

339. UNNAMED coupe dessert plate, 7¾" diameter. Blank: *Diana.* Backmark: H. Color code: All gold decor. H & Co. (7).

341. UNNAMED sugar bowl and cream pitcher for dessert. Sugar bowl, 2¼". Cream pitcher, 3¼" to lip. Blank: *Marseille.* Backmark: B. Color code: Background eight shades lighter than 49 shading to cream. H & Co. (2).

340. PROMISE OF FRUIT plate, 8½" diameter. Blank: *Diana.* Backmark: B. Color code: Flowers, 3, two shades lighter than 4; 42, 25. Foliage, 29, 30, 69, 48, touched with 3. Branches, two and four shades darker than 69. H & Co. (28).

342. PLEASANT HILL plate, 8½" diameter. Blank: *Diana.* Backmark: H. Color code: Flowers one shade darker than 54; 53. Foliage, 29 touched with 16. H & Co. (54).

343. BRANDYWINE VILLAGE demitasse cup and saucer. Saucer, 4¾" diameter. Blank: *Cannelé*. Backmark: B. Color code: Flowers, 54, 23, 13, enameled and touched with white. Foliage, 22, 29, 30. H & Co. (2).

344. GOLDEN DAWN plate, 7½" diameter. Blank: *Marseille*. Backmark: H. Color code: Flowers, gold on background of 6 shading to 10. H & Co. (2).

345. GEORGIA saucer, 5⅜" diameter. Blank: *Eyelet**. Backmark: J. Color code: Flowers, 3, 4, 60, two shades darker than 60, one shade darker than 42. Foliage, 27, 28, 21. H & Co. (15).

346. GREEN VALLEY saucer, 5⅝" diameter. Blank: *Plain*. Backmark: J. Color code: Flowers, 5, 21, two shades lighter than 22. Border, 2 with gold. H & Co. (90).

347. UNNAMED Turkish cup, 1⁷/₈″ high. Blank: *Plain*. Backmark: J. Note: This cup is without any handle! H & Co. (1).

348. UNNAMED saucer, 5½″ diameter. Blank: *Osier*. Backmark: B. Color code: Cavetto lobed in solid color one shade lighter than 51. H & Co. (81).

349. HANOVER saucer, 5³/₈″ diameter. Blank: *Silver*. Backmark: J. Color code: Flowers, 3, 4, white. Foliage, 27, 28 touched with 4. Shadows, 67. H & Co. (28).

350. UNNAMED oyster plate, 9″ diameter. Blank: *Ranson*. Backmark: H. Color code: Gold trim only. H & Co. (2).

351. KILLARNEY CASTLE plate, 8½" diameter. Blank: *Diana.* Backmark: J. Color code: Background, 19 with gold and gold medallion. H & Co. (7).

352. HEREFORD saucer, 5½" diameter. Blank: *Plain.* Backmark: J. Color code: Conventional border in black, 42, 13. H & Co. (17).

353. ALAMEDA plate, 8½" diameter. Blank: *Strasburg.* Backmark: H. Color code: Flowers, 12, 9, 10, 70. Foliage, 69, one shade darker than 70. H & Co. (17).

354. McNEARNEY coupe-shaped dessert plate, 7⁵⁄₈" diameter. Blank: *Ormolu Buckles*.* Backmark: J. Color code: Flowers and foliage, 33, white, two shades lighter than 33; 24, 25, four shades lighter than 57; two shades lighter than 14. Shadows, 5. Border and scallops, 37. H & Co. (53).

355. EMILY saucer, 5½" diameter. Blank: *Plain.* Backmark: B. Color code: Border, 47. Flowers, 7, 1, white. Foliage, two shades lighter than 55; 43, 25. H & Co. (17).

356. PINK POPPY coupe-shaped bread and butter plate, 6¹/₁₆" diameter. Blank: *Ranson.* Backmark: J. Color code: Flowers, 5, 6 outlined in 7. Foliage, 27, two shades darker than 27 touched with 6. H & Co. (3).

357. DAINTY BESS saucer, 5³/₈" diameter. Blank: *Seed Pearls.* Backmark: J. Color code: Flowers, 3, 4, touched with 23. Foliage, four shades lighter than 22 touched with 4. H & Co. (7).

358. CLAYTON plate, 6⁵/₈" diameter. Blank: *Ranson.* Backmark: J. Color code: Flowers and foliage, 5, 59, 60, two shades lighter than 62; 20, 62. H & Co. (17).

359. DORSETSHIRE plate, 7⁷/₈″ diameter. Blank: *Strasburg.* Backmark: H. Color code: Flowers, 3, 4, 42. Foliage, 21, two shades lighter than 21. H & Co. (17).

360. VICTORIA BAY pitcher to washbowl set, 11½″ to tip of spout. Blank: *Plain.* Backmark: A. Color code: Bands three shades darker than 38 with gold. H & Co. (1).

361. MORNING FRESHNESS hot water pitcher, 7½″ to tip of lip. Blank: *Ovide.* Backmark: A. Color code: One and two shades lighter than 36. H & Co. (1).

362. ALICIA plate, 8¾″ diameter. Blank: *Embroidery**. Backmark: J. Color code: Flowers two shades darker than 1; 2 tipped with 42. Foliage two shades darker than 29 tipped with 1. Shadows, 7. H & Co. (6).

363. MAID MARIAN plate, 9½″ diameter. Blank: *Plain*. Backmark: J. Color code: Flowers two shades darker than 8 outlined with 7. Foliage, 24, 34, two shades darker than 8 outlined with 7. H & Co. (1).

364. BERNE saucer, 5³/8″ diameter. Blank: *Ranson*. Backmark: H. Color code: Flowers, 4, 9, 42. Foliage, 18. Shadows, 67, 70. H & Co. (28).

365. LITTLE ROSE tea caddy, 5″ tall. Blank: *Ranson*. Backmark: H. Color code: Foliage, two shades lighter than 40. Tiny outlines, 15. Flowers, 5, 6. H & Co. (1).

366. REEVE plate, 6″ diameter. Blank: *Plain*. Backmark: J. Color code: Flowers and foliage, 5, 6, 7, 11, 20, 34, 22. H & Co. (83).

367. SEAFORD saucer, 5³/₈″ diameter. Blank: *Ranson*. Backmark: J. Color code: Flowers, 3 touched with 4, white and five shades lighter than 3; 4, 53. Foliage, 21 touched with 3 and 42. Shadows, 67. H & Co. (22).

368. APPLE BLOSSOM* bread and butter plate, 6½″ diameter. Blank: *Plain*. Backmark: RR. Color code: Inner circle of gold background color two shades lighter than 23. Flowers, 6 touched in two shades lighter than 23; 70 outlined in 13. Foliage, one shade darker than 20. Shadow, 70. Amer. Theo. (1).

369. SOUTHPORT cup and saucer. Saucer, 4³/₈″ diameter. Blank: *Star*. Backmark: J. Color code: Flowers, 1, 2, 3, 5, 42, 65, 68. Foliage, 18, 23, 30, 1. H & Co. (2).

370. RANDALLSTOWN plate, 9½″ diameter. Blank: *Ranson*. Backmark: J. Color code: Flowers, 5, 6. Foliage, 28. H & Co. (65).

371. THE MONACO* saucer, 5⅝" diameter. Blank: *Plain.* Backmark: J. Color code: Conventional border, 30, 28, outlined in 13. H & Co. (82).

372. FLORINE plate, 6⅛" diameter. Blank: *Diana.* Backmark: J. Color code: Flowers, 1, 2. Foliage, 69. Scrolls, 9, 10. Border, 70. H & Co. (49).

373. LINDA plate, 9¾" diameter. Blank: *Double Scallops*.* Backmark: J. Color code: Design touched with enamel. Flowers, 3, 4 with white, two shades lighter than 53, 50. Foliage, 27, 28 touched with 36. H & Co. (65).

374. BARTLETT plate, 8½" diameter. Blank: *Star.* Backmark: J. Color code: Flowers, 6 touched with 2, 42, white, 66. Foliage one shade lighter than 22 with touches of 42, white, 2. Shadows, 58 touched with 6. H & Co. (1).

375. WESTMORLAND saucer, 5¼" diameter. Blank: *Plain.* Backmark: J. Color code: Cream background with flowers two shades lighter than 2; 62, 56, four shades darker than 56; 60, five shades darker than 42, two shades darker than 48, four shades darker than 44; 12, 62, one shade darker than 44. Foliage, 29, 30, 21. H & Co. (40).

376. POWELL plate, 9½" diameter. Blank: *Strasburg.* Backmark: J. Color code: Flowers, 3, 4 touched with 7. Foliage, two shades darker than 27 touched with 7. H & Co. (12).

377. HARVEY square butter pat, 2¾" diameter. Blank: *Pompadour.* Backmark: B. Color code: Flowers, 3, 4, 42, 67. Foliage, 69 touched with 11. Color code variation: Flowers, 42, 53, 8, 69. Foliage, 9, 16 touched with 36. H & Co. (1).

378. AVIGNON plate, 6⅛" diameter. Blank: *Ranson.* Backmark: J. Color code: Flowers and foliage, 9 touched with 7, 28, 29, 26. H & Co. (35).

379. AULTMAN plate, 9½" diameter. Blank: *Ranson*. Backmark: J. Color code: Flowers, 67 touched with 3, 20, 50, 4. Foliage two shades darker than 21 touched with 3. H & Co. (8).

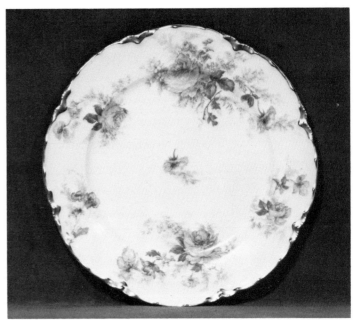

380. AMBROSE bread and butter plate, 6¼" diameter. Blank: *Ranson*. Backmark: J. Color code: Flowers, 6, 10, 23, two shades lighter than 13. Foliage, 29, 27. Shadows, 48. H & Co. (17).

381. ALTHEA plate, 8½" diameter. Blank: *Ranson*. Backmark: J. Color code: Flowers, 58, 61. Foliage, 20 touched with 2. Shadows, 1. H & Co. (65).

382. AUTUMN EVENING plate, 8¾" diameter. Blank: *Silver*. Backmark: J. Color code: Flowers, 59, five shades lighter than 11. Foliage, 28, 27. Shadows, 67, 70. H & Co. (81).

383. ALICE plate, 9¾" diameter. Blank: *Pompadour II.* Backmark: J. Color code: Flowers, 3 touched with 24, 60, 65. Foliage, 29. H & Co. (65).

384. HARPER'S FERRY saucer, 5⅜" diameter. Blank: *Embroidery**. Backmark: J. Color code: Flowers, white with shades of 5, 6, touched with 2. Foliage, 21 touched with 2 and white; 67 touched with 2. Scroll, 20, 21 touched with 2, 6, 67. H & Co. (1).

385. SALLY LOUTHAN cup and saucer. Saucer, 5¾" diameter. Blank: *Nenuphar, Plain**. Backmark: H. Color code: Flowers, 60, 63. Foliage, 20. H & Co. (55).

386. MAUREEN cup and saucer. Saucer, 5⅝" diameter. Platter, 12⅜" by 8⅝". Blank: *Star.* Backmark: J. Color code: Flowers, 60, 59, 56, 1, 10. Foliage two shades darker than 21; 60 touched with 1. H & Co. (30).

387. WOODCLIFF plate, 8½" diameter. Blank: *Seed Pearls**. Backmark: J. Color code: Flowers, 1, three shades lighter than 2; 25, 59, 60. Foliage, 20, 21. Border two shades darker than 21; gold. H & Co. (65).

388. CHRISTINA saucer, 5³/₈" diameter. Blank: *Gabrielle**. Backmark: J. Color code: Flowers, 3, 4, two shades lighter than 2. Foliage, 20. H & Co. (37).

389. MANZANO salad plate, 8" diameter. Blank: *Pompadour.* Backmark: I. Color code: Edge gold-dotted with gold leaf pattern. Flowers, 65 touched in 14 and three shades darker than 69; centers, 42. Small flower, white striped in 2 and outlined in 2. Foliage, 69 and darker shades of 69 touched in 2. Small flowers, 42 and white. H & Co. (2).

390. ANN ARBOR bread and butter plate, 6¼" diameter. Blank: *Plain.* Backmark: J. Color code: Flowers, 2, 1, two shades darker than 1, 48. Foliage, 22, 28 touched with 4. H & Co. (17).

391. BRAHMS dinner plate, 9¾" diameter. Blank: *Ranson.* Backmark: J. Color code: Rim brushed with gold on ½" border of cobalt with gold enamel floral wreath on inner edge. Flowers, 42, two shades lighter than 2 (some are tipped with gold), 63, 53, white. Foliage, 20, 21. H & Co. (33).

392. CELESTE plate, 8½" diameter. Blank: *Diana.* Backmark: H. Color code: Flowers and foliage, 8 touched with four shades lighter than 15. Shadows, 70. H & Co. (81).

393. SEGOVIA plate, 7⅛" diameter. Blank: *Cannelé.* Backmark: B. Color code: Flowers, 42, 53, 13, 69, 5, 15. Foliage, 68, 69, 46. H & Co. (2).

394. LOTUS BLOSSOM saucer and ramekin. Saucer, 4⅛". Blank: *Star.* Backmark: J. Color code: Flowers two shades lighter than 3; 3 touched with 23, 40. Foliage, 20, 21. H & Co. (34).

396. WILLIAMS demitasse saucer, 5″ diameter. Blank: *Napkin Fold*. Backmark: B. Color code: Five shades darker than 2. H & Co. (1).

395. UPSALA coupe-shaped dessert plate, 7½″ diameter. Blank: *Ranson*. Backmark: J. Color code: Flowers, 3, 5, 6, white. Foliage, 20, three shades lighter than 20. Shadows, 67. H & Co. (53).

398. SPRINGTIME* bread and butter plate, 6¾″ diameter. Blank: *Plain*. Backmark: RR. Color code: Flowers, 9 touched with 2; 5 touched with 2 and white; 63 touched with 2; centers 41 and white; 60 touched with 41, 2. Foliage, 20, 23, 36 touched in 2. Border rim background two shades lighter than 23. Amer. Theo. 1 (1).

397. TARANTELLA plate, 8³/₈″ diameter. Blank: *Cannelé*. Backmark: B. Color code: Flowers, 1 touched with 2 and ten shades lighter than 49, four shades lighter than 55, 22. H & Co. (15).

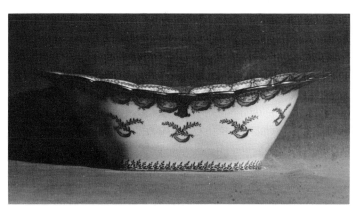

399. RANDALIA bowl, 10″ wide by 3″ tall. Blank: *Crescent.* Backmark: H. Color code: Ribbon, 21, 22. Other decoration, gold. H & Co. (2).

400. PEPPER FLOWER butter pat, 3¹/₈″ diameter. Blank: *Ruby.* Backmark: J. Color code: Flowers, 47. Foliage two shades darker than 40 outlined in 47. H & Co. (1).

401. ADRIENNE tray, 6⁷/₈″ by 8³/₄″. Blank: *Ranson.* Backmark: H. Color code: Flowers, two shades lighter than 1 outlined in 13. Foliage, 20 touched with 15. H & Co. (1).

402. BRENTWOOD saucer, 5³/₈″ diameter. Blank: *Star.* Backmark: J. Color code: Flowers, 3, 5, three shades lighter than 2; 56, 66, 42. Foliage, 18. H & Co. (12).

403. MORNING GLORY soup bowl, 7½" diameter. Blank: *Crow's-foot**. Backmark: J. Color code: Flowers, 3 touched with three shades lighter than 2. Foliage, 27, 28 touched with 4. H & Co. (35).

404. LEAH dinner plate, 9⅝" diameter. Blank: *Plain*. Backmark: J. Color code: Bands, 1/16" gold on rim, 1/8" gold inner. Flowers, enameled, lighter shades of 2 touched in 26, 22, and white; white touched in 26, 22 and shades of 2. Foliage, 22 touched in 26 and 5. Foliage, shadow one shade lighter than 25. H & Co. (65).

405. WOOD'S HOLE candy dish, 6⅝" diameter. Blank: *Silver*. Backmark: J. Color code: Flowers, 42, one shade lighter than 42, 4, 3, white touched with 3. Foliage two shades darker than 21; 24, three shades lighter than 22. H & Co. (56).

406. MOBILE bowl, 5" diameter. Blank: *Plain*. Backmark: J. Color code: Conventional border, gold and 22. Note: Decorator's mark in gold—custom made. H & Co. (28).

407. CLASSIC plate, 6³/₁₆" diameter. Blank: *Plain.* Backmark: J. Color code: Large flowers, 3, 9. Small flowers two shades darker than 42. Foliage, 28; 28 touched with three shades lighter than 2, 7. Scrolls, 56. H & Co. (12).

408. ARMISTEAD chocolate saucer, 4⁷/₈" diameter. Blank: *Plain.* Backmark: J. Color code: Edge, brushed gold ¹/₁₆" band in one shade lighter than 55. Gold flowers and foliage in three bands in center of saucer. Flowers, 42 touched with white, 2 touched with white, six small flowers two shades lighter than 57 with centers of 2. Foliage one shade darker than 35 touched with 2, 6, 57. Stems, 57, 35. Shadows, 59 touched with 4. H & Co. (1).

409. WELLESLEY* plate, 9³/₄" diameter. Blank: *Plain.* Backmark: J. Color code: ³/₁₆" wide gold border engraved in loosely twisted rope with quatrofoils in the interstices. Note: The exception to the plates trimmed only in gold being nameless is obviated if factory-named. H & Co. (1).

410. ORIENT dinner plate, 9½" diameter. Blank: *Plain.* Backmark: J. Color code: Flowers, 8 and black. Scrolls two shades darker than 43. H & Co. (17).

411. NELL DORR cup and saucer. Saucer, 4⁷⁄₈″ diameter. Blank: *Bowknots**. Backmark: J. Color code: Flowers, 62, 63, shades of 3 and 70. Stems two shades darker than 21. H & Co. (70).

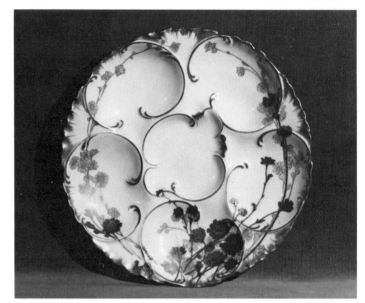

412. MAGDALENA oyster plate, 8½″ diameter. Blank: *Unknown.* Backmark: H. Color code: Background cream or four shades lighter than 23. Flowers, 13 with gold. Foliage, 36 with gold. H & Co. (2).

413. KATIE cream pitcher, 3″ to lip. Blank: *Plain.* Backmark: B. Color code: Flowers, 42, 59, 60. Foliage, 29. Shadows, 68. H & Co. (1).

414. JOELLEN saucer, 5³⁄₈″ diameter. Blank: *Plain.* Backmark: J. Color code: Flowers, 5, 6, white. Foliage, 20, 21. Shadows, 67. H & Co. (28).

415. ISABEL fruit dish, 5″ diameter. Blank: *Plain.* Backmark: J. Color code: Conventional border two shades lighter than 22. Scallops, 41. Flowers two shades lighter than 57, 47. H & Co. (7).

416. HELENE* saucer, 6″ diameter. Blank: *Romeo.* Backmark: RR. Color code: Flowers, 43 touched with white, 2 and 69; 69 touched with white and 2. Foliage, 69 touched with white, 21, and 2. Amer. Theo. (1).

417. GARDEN FLOWERS* bread and butter plate, 6¾″ diameter. Blank: *Plain.* Backmark: RR. Color code: Border flowers shades of 2 touched in white with 64 centers. Buds, 64, 6. Border, 20 touched in 22 and black. Center flowers shades of 5 and 6 touched with three shades lighter than 2 and white and black. Flowers, 64 touched with black, white, 20 and 22. Flowers, 32 with 2 and 42 centers, touched in white, black and 21. Flowers, 2, 5, 6 touched in 16, 42, black, white. Foliage shades of 25, 21, 22 touched in black. Border rim background two shades lighter than 23. Amer. Theo. (1).

418. FLEUR-DE-LYS cocoa pot, 7½″ to lip. Blank: *Marseille.* Backmark: H. Color code: Gold, 53. H & Co. (2).

419. JUNO egg cup, 3¼" tall. Blank: Pedestal, *Plain*. Backmark: J. Color code: Foliage, 2, 9, 30 touched with 4. Flowers, 64, 65, 41, 14, 3. H & Co. (1).

420. DEANNA plate, 9⅝" diameter. Blank: *Marseille*. Backmark: H. Color code: Flowers and foliage, 5, 70. Shadows, 67. H & Co. (3).

421. CANBY saucer, 5½" diameter. Blank: *Plain.* Backmark: J. Color code: Flowers, 6, white, 2. Berries, 2. Foliage, one shade lighter than 22 touched with 2. H & Co. (1).

422. BERMUDA saucer, 5½" diameter. Blank: *Silver*. Backmark: J. Color code: Flowers, 1, two shades darker than 1 and white, 64, 61. Foliage, two shades darker than 21, 20. H & Co. (17).

424. DIRECTOIRE plate, 8½" diameter. Blank: *Fluted Ruffle**. Backmark: J. Color code: Flowers, 1 touched with enamel. Foliage, 18. H & Co. (65).

423. ANNEAU DE ROSE tray, 11¼ diameter. Blank: *Plain.* Backmark: J. Color code: Flowers, touched with enamel; 3, 4, 67. Foliage, 20, 21 touched with 6. H & Co. (1).

425. COLBY cup and saucer. Saucer, 4½" diameter. Blank: *Plain.* Backmark: B. Color code: Flowers, 42 outlined in 15. Foliage, 70 outlined in 15, 2. H & Co. (2).

426. CHARLESTON open vegetable bowl, 9½" wide by 2" tall. Blank: *Palme.* Backmark: J. Color code: Flowers, 3, 6, 2 touched with 3, white, white enamel. Foliage, 20, 23, 3. H & Co. (2).

427. LAKE GEORGE plate, 6¼" diameter. Blank: *Plain.* Backmark: J. Color code: Flowers, 8, 4, three shades lighter than 2, 42. Foliage, 22, two shades lighter than 22 touched with 42. H & Co. (56).

428. WOODBRIDGE plate, 8¾" diameter. Blank: *Double Scallops*.* Backmark: J. Color code: Flowers, two and three shades darker than 1; 41, 42, 59. Foliage, 30 touched with white. Berries, 15. H & Co. (65).

429. LARCHMONT plate, 6¼" diameter. Blank: *Crow'sfoot.* Backmark: J. Color code: Conventional border, 22 and gold. H & Co. (12).

430. MIAMI plate, 8½" diameter. Blank: *Star.* Backmark: J. Color code: Flowers, 42 touched with 1, 2; 1 touched with 42; four shades lighter than 57. Foliage, 21, 22 touched with 23 and 66. Shadows, 59. H & Co. (37).

431. ROSE SNOWFLAKE plate, 7½" diameter. Blank: *Plain.*
Backmark: J. Color code: Flowers, 3, 4 shading to white. Foliage, 27,
28. H & Co. (12).

432. L'AUTOMNE cup and saucer. Saucer, 5¼" diameter. Blank:
Pompadour. Backmark: C. Color code: Flowers one shade lighter
than 64, one shade lighter and one shade darker than 47. Foliage, 70, 2,
42. Handle, gold. H & Co. (2).

433. O'MALLEY dessert plate, 7⅝" diameter. Blank: *Plain.*
Backmark: J. Color code: Gold conventional border and 21, 41, 13. H
& Co. (17).

434. LILY OF THE VALLEY covered mayonnaise bowl lid, 4¾" to tip
of finial. Blank: *Marseille.* Backmark: H. Color code: Flowers, 5, 6,
9. Foliage, 68 outlined with 15. H & Co. (1).

221

435. OLGA salad plate, 7½″ diameter. Blank: *Plain.* Backmark: J. Color code: Conventional border, 21, 13. H & Co. (17).

436. CAROL saucer, 5³/₈″ diameter. Blank: *Ranson.* Backmark: J. Color code: Flowers two shades darker and two shades lighter than 7. Foliage two and three shades lighter than 27; 47. H & Co. (81).

437. FINESSE saucer, 5³/₈″ diameter. Blank: *Plain.* Backmark: J. Color code: Flowers, 67 touched with eight shades lighter than 15. Foliage, 27, 28. Scrolls two shades darker than 5. H & Co. (15).

438. FAIRFIELD cup and saucer. Saucer, 4¼″ diameter. Blank: *Marseille.* Backmark: H. Color code: Flowers and foliage two shades darker than 20, 68, two shades lighter than 15. H & Co. (2).

222

439. FORT SUMNER plate, 9¾" diameter. Blank: *Plain.* Backmark: J. Color code: Conventional border three shades darker than 9, 3, 41, 6, 35, 53, 21, 66 and white. H & Co. (40).

440. FOUNTAIN three-piece butter server with insert. Plate, 8½" diameter. Cover, 4" tall. Blank: *Unknown.* Backmark: J. Color code: Border two shades darker than 11; 21. Circle, 15, black, 21, 36, 2, white. Water spray, 53. H & Co. (2).

441. MAPLE CANYON plate, 8¾" diameter. Blank: *Silver.* Backmark: J. Color code: Flowers, 4, 8, 10. Foliage 28. Shadows, 10. H & Co. (37).

442. FANTASY saucer, 5¼" diameter. Blank: *Marseille.* Backmark: B. Color code: Background in cream. Flowers, 54, 42 touched with 12. Foliage, 21. H & Co. (7).

443. CORFU saucer, 5³/₈″ diameter. Blank: *Seed Pearls**. Backmark: J. Color code: Flowers, 41, 42 shading to white touched with 50, white touched with 50, 42. Foliage two shades lighter than 22 touched with 1 and 42. H & Co. (1).

444. SPRINGER cup and saucer. Saucer 5³/₄″ diameter. Blank: *Star*. Backmark: J. Color code: Flowers, 42, 4, one shade darker than 4, one shade lighter than 32 outlined in three shades lighter than 57. Foliage, 25 touched with 4. Shadows, 24. H & Co. (56).

445. MARJORIE saucer, 4¼″ diameter. Blank: *Silver*. Backmark: J. Color code: Border, cobalt and gold. Flowers one and two shades darker and lighter than 1, 5, 42, 46, 59. Foliage, 20, 21. H & Co. (65).

446. ZERMATT plate, 9³/₈″ diameter. Blank: *Pompadour*. Backmark: I. Color code: Conventional grain border in gold. Flowers and foliage five shades lighter than 14, 65, 28, 29. H & Co. (28).

447. CELEBRATION plate, 8¾" diameter. Blank: *Plain.* Backmark: J. Color code: Flowers two shades lighter than 2, 5, one shade lighter than 42, 52, five shades lighter than 57, 4. Foliage, 20, 21 touched with 11. H & Co. (81).

448. MAIDSTONE plate, 6¼" diameter. Blank: *Star.* Backmark: J. Color code: Flowers, 41, 42, 1, three shades lighter than 2, 10. Foliage, 22 touched with three shades lighter than 2, 42. Shadows, 10. H & Co. (12).

449. ANGELIQUE saucer 4³/₈" diameter. Blank: *Double Scallops**. Backmark: J. Color code: Flowers, 1, 4, white. Foliage, 28 touched with 4. H & Co. (80).

450. BRUGES dinner plate, 9½" diameter. Blank: *Ranson.* Backmark: J. Color code: Flowers, 1, white, 42 touched with 13. Foliage, 19, white touched with 4. H & Co. (17).

451. WHEELER service plate, 10³/₈″ diameter. Blank: *Plain.* Backmark: J, factory number 34119. Color code: Border and central medallion, 11, 42. H & Co. (17).

452. LARSEN plate, 9³/₄″ diameter. Blank: *Seed Pearls**. Backmark: J. Color code: Scalloped border heavily embossed gold with conventional gold design within. Flowers, white, 70, heavy white enamel. Touched with two shades lighter than 2, 3, three shades deeper than 3; centers 29 touched with 8. Foliage, 30, 29, 25 touched with 8. Shadows, 68. H & Co. (52).

453. COPENHAGEN saucer, 4³/₈″ diameter. Blank: *Plain.* Backmark: J. Color code: Conventional border, bows, 40 and shades lighter touched with 4, 3. H & Co. (15).

454. SOUTHERN BELLE cup, 3⁵/₈″ diameter. Blank: *Plain.* Backmark: C. Color code: Flowers, 57, two shades lighter than 57, 1, two shades lighter than 2, 4, 11. Foliage, 22, 28, 27. (Note roped handle.) H & Co. (40).

455. SIENNA luncheon plate, 8⁵/₈″ diameter. Blank: *Silver.* Backmark: J. Color code: Flowers, 28, 27 touched with 3, 10. Foliage, 28, 27, 4. H & Co. (81).

456. LATE BLOOMS saucer, 5½″ diameter. Blank: *Plain.* Backmark: B. Color code: Flowers, 44 with 65, 8, 15. Foliage, 44 with 65, 8, 15. H & Co. (15).

457. WEEDEN punch cup, 3⁷/₈″ by 3″. Blank: *Ranson.* Backmark: J. Color code: Gold trim. Ribbon three shades lighter than 28, outlined in 13. Flowers, 13. Foliage 30. H & Co. (2).

458. LADY SLIPPER saucer, 6¼″ diameter. Blank: *Diana.* Backmark: H. Color code: Background, 48 increasing in depth. Foliage, 36 with gold. H & Co. (7).

459. BUTTERNUT TREE saucer, 5⁷/₈″ diameter. Blank: *Plain.*
Backmark: B. Color code: Flowers, 15, 56, touches of 28. H & Co.
(3).

460. THE TARANTO* plate, 9⁵/₈″ diameter. Blank: *Marseille.* Backmark: J. Color code: Flowers, 34, 35, 15. Foliage, 28, four shades
lighter than 30. Shadows, 18. H & Co. (1).

461. PEDERANALES butter dish insert, 4⁹/₁₆″ diameter. Blank: *Plain.*
Backmark: J. Color code: Flowers, 64 touched with 15, 5; 5 touched
with 64 and white. Foliage, 21 touched with 15. H & Co. (1).

462. ART NOUVEAU saucer, 5³/₈″ diameter. Blank: *Plain.* Backmark: J. Color code: Scrolls two shades lighter than 55. Flowers two
shades darker than 42. Foliage, 20 touched with 43. H & Co. (1).

463. WALSTON saucer, 4⅝″ diameter. Blank: *Silver.* Backmark: J. Color code: Border, cobalt with gold. Flowers, 1, 61, 9, 63. Foliage, 20, 21. H & Co. (65).

464. UNNAMED plate, 8¾″ diameter. Blank: *Pompadour.* Backmark: B. Color code: All gold trim. H & Co. (71).

465. SAN ANTONIO plate, 9¾″ diameter. Blank: *Plain.* Backmark: J. Color code: Background color one shade darker than 5. Flowers white, one shade lighter than 21 touched with 45, 3, 4. Foliage, 22, three and four shades lighter than 22 touched with 4. H & Co. (12).

466. UNNAMED coffeepot. Base ¾″ wide, 9¾″ to top of finial. Blank: *Plain.* Backmark: B with English Registry mark. Color code: Gold trim. (Note braided handle.) H & Co. (1).

467. ORPHA plate, 8½" diameter. Blank: *Ranson.* Backmark: B. Color code: Medallions, gold and black. Flowers, 6, 7 fading to white, 43. Foliage, 28, 29 touched with 4. Note: This has a gold factory number, #30799, indicating a special order. Also note the gold brushing with the *Ranson* border. H & Co. (7).

468. UNNAMED cup and saucer. Saucer, 5⅛" diameter. Blank: *Saxon-on-Claws.* Backmark: H. Color code: Gold trim only. H & Co. (56).

469. GIRARD saucer, 5⅜" diameter. Blank: *Ranson.* Backmark: J. Color code: Band, gold, then 37. Flowers, 3, 4, white. Foliage, 22, white, tipped with 4, 63. H & Co. (56).

470. CLAYMONT saucer, 5½" diameter. Blank: *Plain.* Backmark: J. Color code: Flowers, 2, 6 touched with 26. Foliage, 21 touched with 6, 26, 15. Shadow, 26 touched with 15. H & Co. (1).

471. MARY ANN saucer, 5 ³/₈" diameter. Blank: *Ranson.* Backmark: J. Color code: Flowers, 3 and one shade darker, one shade lighter than 3. Foliage, 26 and one shade darker and one shade lighter than 26. H & Co. (15).

472. ALLEGRO teacup and saucer. Saucer, 5½" diameter. Blank: *Star.* Backmark: J. Color code: Conventional border one shade darker than 29 outlined in 13. Inner border of cup, 29, 30 outlined in 13. H & Co. (33).

473. BRIDESMAID'S BOUQUET saucer, 5" diameter. Blank: *Diana.* Backmark: H. Color code: Flowers, 5, 6. Foliage, 28. Ribbon, 63. H & Co. (28).

474. CHLOE cup and saucer. Saucer, 4¾" diameter. Blank: *Osier.* Backmark: E. Color code: Flowers, 61, 62, 2, 42, 13, 9. Foliage, 22, 53. H & Co. (2).

475. SHANNON plate, 7 3/8″ diameter. Blank: *Plain.* Backmark: B.
Color code: Flowers and foliage, 37, 63, two shades darker than 48, 9.
H & Co. (28).

476. BEAUFORT plate, 8 3/8″ diameter. Blank: *Diana.* Backmark: J.
Color code: Conventional border, 18 outlined in three shades darker
than 48. Flowers, 9, two shades lighter than 1, 23, 25. Foliage, 18, 21.
H & Co. (15).

477. BELLINGHAM saucer, 5 3/8″ diameter. Blank: *Plain.* Backmark:
J. Color code: Conventional border, 29, 30, 12. H & Co. (35).

478. BLUEWATER LAKE butter dish insert, 4½″ diameter. Blank:
Plain. Backmark: H. Color code: Flowers, 56 touched with 13.
Foliage, 20 touched with 13. H & Co. (1).

479. BETTY saucer, 5 3/8" diameter. Blank: *Silver.* Backmark: J. Color code: Lappet border, 42 outlined in black. Flowers, 57, one shade lighter than 57, 42, 48, 49, 45. Foliage, touches of 22. H & Co. (76).

480. BUCHAREST plate, 6¼" diameter. Blank: *Plain.* Backmark: J. Color code: Conventional border, gold and 29. H & Co. (12).

481. BRANDENBURG butter pat, 3" diameter. Blank: *Portia.* Backmark: J. Color code: Flowers, 5 touched with 2, 65 and 42. Centers, 65 touched with 2, white, and three shades darker of 65. Foliage, 20, 21, touched with 2, 65 and white. H & Co. (1).

482. ERNESTINE salad plate, 7½" diameter. Blank: *Plain.* Backmark: J. Color code: Flowers, 9, two shades lighter than 57, 43. Foliage, 27 outlined in two shades lighter than 57. H & Co. (12).

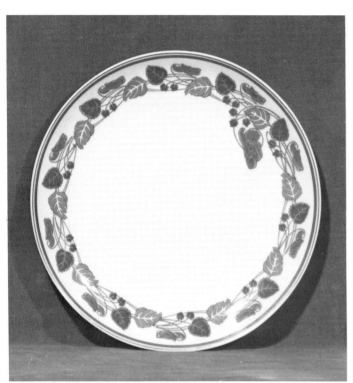

483. STEWART coupe-shaped plate, 8½" diameter. Blank: *Plain.* Backmark: J. Color code: Flowers three shades lighter than 2 outlined in 13. Foliage, 30, two shades lighter than 40 outlined in 13. H & Co. (53).

484. MARIANNA plate, 9¾" diameter. Blank: *Double Scallops**. Backmark: J. Color code: Flowers two to three shades darker than 1. Foliage, 29. H & Co. (65).

485. WARNER tureen with plate. Tureen, 8¾" wide, 6" tall. Plate, 9⅛" diameter. Blank: *Crow'sfoot.* Backmark: J. Color code: Conventional border, gold, 20. Flowers, 66, 55, 3, 4. Snowflake medallion, gold. H & Co. (20).

486. LOIS HUDSON BEEBEE teacup saucer, 5⅞" diameter. Blank: *Ranson.* Backmark: J. Color code: Flowers and foliage, 6, 21, white, touches of 45, touches of one shade lighter than 13, 35. Note: This pattern was collected in Iowa, one piece at a time, by the owner's grandmother for whom it is named. H & Co. (25).

487. UTICA saucer, 5 3/8″ diameter. Blank: *Plain.* Backmark: J. Color code: Flowers, 6, 5, white, 63. Foliage, 30, one, two, and three shades lighter than 30 touched with 6. H & Co. (17).

488. WESLEY saucer, 5 3/8″ diameter. Blank: *Plain.* Backmark: J. Color code: Conventional border, 17, 42. H & Co. (78).

489. TUOLUMNE MEADOWS plate, 7½″ diameter. Blank: *Plain.* Backmark: J. Color code: Flowers, 4, 3, 1. Foliage, one shade darker than 21 touched with 4. Shadows, 68. H & Co. (12).

490. STARLIGHT platter, 7¾″ long. Blank: *Pompadour.* Backmark: I. Color code: Flowers one shade lighter than 64, one shade darker than 47. Foliage, 70, 2, 42. H & Co. (2).

491. RELDON saucer, 5 1/8" diameter. Blank: *Plain*. Backmark: J. Color code: Conventional border, 42, black. H & Co. (12).

492. PICKERING cup and saucer. Saucer, 5¼" diameter. Blank: *Plain*. Backmark: J. Color code: Flowers, two shades lighter than 52, 5 touched with 13. Foliage, 28. H & Co. (56).

493. OLD SOUTH saucedish, 5 3/8" diameter. Blank: *Plain*. Backmark: J. Color code: Flowers, 4, 3, 23. Foliage, 20 tipped with 4. H & Co. (15).

494. NORWOOD plate, 9¾" diameter. Blank: *Plain*. Backmark: J. Color code: Conventional border of leaf swags and beads in 12, 28. Flowers, 3, 4, 8, white. Foliage, 27, 28 touched with 3. H & Co. (40).

495. MAGDALENA cup and saucer. Saucer, 5¼" diameter. Blank: *Diana*. Backmark: B. Color code: Background ten shades lighter than 55 shading to blue-white. Flowers, 36. Foliage, 39. H & Co. (6).

496. KELLY vegetable dish lid, 8⁷/₈" diameter. Blank: *Silver*. Backmark: J. Color code: Flowers, 9 touched with 13, one shade lighter than 30. Foliage one shade lighter than 30 touched with 13. H & Co. (1).

497. JACQUELINE plate, 8⁵/₈" diameter. Blank: *Plain*. Backmark: J. Color code: Flowers, 2, 5, 6, 42, 23. Foliage, 36 shading to white, 23. Border, 66 with gold tracing. H & Co. (2).

498. HARVEST GLORY coffeepot, 8" to lip. Blank: *Triangle*. Backmark: B plus incised English Registry mark. Color code: Flowers, 61, 2 on white. Foliage, 20, 30, 15. Base of body and part of spout, 64 with gold. (Note cable or braided handle.) H & Co. (2).

499. GAINSBOROUGH* saucer, 5⅞" diameter. Blank: *Plain.*
Backmark: TT. Color code: Rim, ¼" gold band inside rim. Flowers,
5, 6, touched in 2; 66 with 57. Centers, 6, 43 outlined with 2. Foliage,
21, 22 touched in 2. Amer. Theo. (1).

500. FRANCIS W. ATKINSON plate, 9⅝" diameter. Blank: *Palme.*
Backmark: J. Color code: Enameled. Border, 2. Flowers, 41, 42, 43,
two shades darker than 46. Foliage, 27 tipped with 22. Shadows, two
shades lighter than 22. H & Co. (6).

501. POTPOURRI luncheon plate, 8⅜" diameter. Blank: *Diana.*
Backmark: B. Color code: Flowers two shades darker than 32, 5, 14.
Foliage two shades darker than 32, 5, 14. H & Co. (3).

502. UNNAMED saucer, 5¼" diameter. Blank: coupe *Diana.* Backmark: H. Color code: Gold only. H & Co. (15).

503. LOFTUS beanery, 3" wide, 6" long. Blank: *Ranson.* Backmark:
J. Color code: Flowers, 63 outlined with 15. Foliage, 18, 19, 15. H &
Co. (1).

504. MOONLIGHT plate, 8½" diameter. Blank: *Diana.* Backmark:
B. Color code: Flowers, 9, 10. Foliage eight shades lighter than 37
touched with white. H & Co. (56).

505. SANTA BARBARA plate, 7½" diameter. Blank: *Plain.*
Backmark: J. Color code: Flowers, 4, 3, 59, 60, white. Foliage, 21.
Shadows, 70. H & Co. (12).

506. BARRY miniature pitcher, 4¼" tall. Blank: *Plain* with anchor
handle. Backmark: GG, English Registry mark, and ¼ pint. Color
code: Band, 65 on 23. Flowers and foliage, 14, two shades darker than
10. H & Co. (2).

507. BLOOMINGDALE saucer, 5³/₈" diameter. Blank: *Basketweave (Osier)*. Backmark: J. Color code: Flowers, 13, 6. Foliage, 21. Bows three shades deeper than 46. H & Co. (15).

508. ARIADNE fruit bowl, 5½" diameter. Blank: *Diana*. Backmark: J. Color code: Conventional border, gold on cobalt. H & Co. (44).

509. VIVIAN teacup, standard size. Blank: *Star*. Backmark: J. Color code: Flowers, 3, 4, white. Foliage, 28. Shadows, 59. H & Co. (17).

510. MELISSA boudoir tray, 8" by 10". Blank: *Unknown*. Backmark: H. Color code: Flowers, 5, 6, 2. Foliage, 20, 21 touched with 2, 53, 67, 68. H & Co. (2).

511. SUE bread and butter plate, 6¹/₈" diameter. Blank: *Double Scallops**. Backmark: J. Color code: Rim, brushed gold. Flowers, 2, 3, 64, 42, white, 68. Foliage, 25, white, 42, 3, 15, 64, 30. Shadows, 67, 70. H & Co. (54).

512. POJOAQUE saucer, 5½" diameter. Blank: *Ranson*. Backmark: J. Color code: Flowers, 7, 6, 5, 63 touched with 6, 28. Foliage, 28. H & Co. (17).

513. EILEEN covered vegetable dish, 9" by 6¼". Blank: *Plain*. Backmark: C. Color code: Band, ³/₈" of 35. Flowers and foliage four shades darker than 60, 54; two shades darker than 52, 7; one shade lighter than 7; two shades lighter than 57, 25, 15, 30. (Note braided handles on bowl and cover.) H & Co. (84).

514. ELMIRA plate, 9½" diameter. Blank: *Ranson*. Backmark: J. Color code: Flowers, 5, 26. Foliage, 27, 28, 29. H & Co. (56).

516. NEW DELHI saucer, 5¾" diameter. Blank: *Nenuphar Plain**. Backmark: J. Color code: Flowers two shades lighter than 41, 42; three shades lighter than 4. Foliage, 27, 28, three shades lighter than 13, 70. H & Co. (81).

515. DAGMAR pickle dish, 8½" by 5". Blank: *Star*. Backmark: J. Color code: Berries, 11, 21. Foliage, 20, 21 touched with 11. H & Co. (1).

517. MASON cup and saucer. Cup, 3¼" diameter, 2" high. Saucer, 5³/₈" diameter. Blank: *Plain*. Backmark: J. Color code: Flowers, 3 edged with 11. Foliage, 26 edged in gold. H & Co. (46).

518. MANHATTAN plate, 9¾" diameter. Blank: *Ruby*. Backmark: J. Color code: Conventional border, 56, gold. Flowers, 4, 3, white. Stems and foliage, 21, one shade lighter than 21, one shade darker than 21 touched with 3. Background for floral wreath one shade darker than 34. H & Co. (12).

519. MAURITANIA luncheon plate, 8½″ diameter. Blank: *Saxon*. Backmark: H. Color code: Flowers two shades lighter than 47, 46, 9, 3, 10. Foliage, 28, 26. H & Co. (15).

520. MT. TAMALPAIS saucer, 5¼″ diameter. Blank: *Star*. Backmark: J. Color code: Flowers, 4, 3, 54, touches of 21, 42. Foliage, 22. H & Co. (1).

521. PYRENEES saucer, 5⅜″ diameter. Blank: *Star*. Backmark: J. Color code: Flowers, shaded 53 and touched with 2. Foliage, 19 touched with 53 and 2. H & Co. (15).

522. YOUNG salad plate, 7½″ diameter. Blank: *Marseille*. Backmark: H. Color code: Flowers, 20, 15, two shades lighter than 28. Foliage, 20. H & Co. (17).

523. MIMI saucer, 4³/₈″ diameter. Blank: *Ranson.* Backmark: J. Color code: Flowers, 4, 3, white. Foliage, 28, white. Stems, 28, two shades lighter than 2. Shadows, 26. H & Co. (28).

524. ST. LAMBERT plate, 6¼″ diameter. Blank: *Silver.* Backmark: J. Color code: Flowers, 6, 8 touched with 7. Foliage, 26, 27, 23. H & Co. (12).

525. BLUE ROSETTE pitcher, 5⁷/₈″ tall to lip. Blank: *Plain.* Backmark: B plus English Registry mark. Color code: Touched with enamel. Flowers and foliage, 48, 49, 63, 64. H & Co. (1).

526. EDENDERRY soup bowl, 9″ diameter. Blank: *Silver.* Backmark: J. Color code: Flowers and foliage, 25, 27, 5, 35, 13. H & Co. (56).

527. EVESHAM saucer, 5½" diameter. Blank: *Crow'sfoot.* Back-mark: J. Color code: Conventional border, 28, 30. Flowers, two shades darker than 8. Foliage, 27. H & Co. (15).

528. EVENING DRESS cup and saucer. Saucer, 4¹¹/₁₆" diameter. Blank: *Plain.* Backmark: J. Color code: Between two bands of Wellsley in gold is leaf design on pale cream background. H & Co. (1).

529. EVANGELINE square butter pat, 2¾". Blank: *Pompadour.* Backmark: B. Color code: Flowers and foliage, 18, 40, 48, 30 outlined with 47. H & Co. (1).

530 (left). CARALISA oyster plate, 7¼" diameter. Blank: *Unknown.* Salesman's sample with unusual backmark—stamped B plus the follow-ing: (88) 1808 Cannelé . . . T. 54 other shapes . . . T.53 (plus) centers. Color code: Shells, gold trim. Flowers, gold, 61, 62, 4, 6, 14. Foliage, 1, 15, 69. Butterfly, 9, 14. H & Co. (1).

530 (right). AT SEA oyster plate, 7¼" diameter. Blank: *Unknown.* Salesman's sample with unusual backmark—stamped B plus the follow-ing (89) 2335 f 6 shells 4.00, 5 shells 3.50, 4 shells 3.25. Color code: Fish and foliage, all gold. Background one shade lighter than 20. H & Co. (1).

531. MEDALLION plate, 9⁵/₈" diameter. Blank: *Ranson.* Backmark: J. Color code: Flowers three shades darker than 5. Foliage, 27, 28. H & Co. (7).

532. ANGEL FIRE cocoa pot, 7³/₄" to lip. Blank: *Pompadour.* Backmark: I. Color code: Flowers and foliage, 37, 42, two shades darker than 9, two shades lighter than 15. Shadow flowers and foliage, 70, two shades darker than 10. H & Co. (2).

533. BURNISHED COPPER plate, 7³/₈" diameter. Blank: *Diana.* Backmark: H. Color code: Background, shades of 13. Foliage, gold. H & Co. (6).

534. CAPE ELIZABETH oyster plate, 7¼" diameter. Blank: *Cannelé.* Backmark: I. Color code: Flowers, 15, 48, 13, 53. Foliage, 15, 53, 13, 14. H & Co. (2).

535. STELLA cake plate, 10¹/₈″ diameter. Blank: *Star.* Backmark: J. Color code: Flowers and foliage, three shades lighter than 2, 23, 24, 8. H & Co. (84).

536. LONGVIEW saucer, 5½″ diameter. Blank: *Ranson.* Backmark: J. Color code: Flowers and foliage, 5, 34, 63, 21, two shades lighter than 13. H & Co. (17).

537. VICTORIANA pin tray, 6¹/₈″ by 5″. Blank: *Club du Barry.* Backmark: I. Color code: Background, Buada Rose bisque. Flowers, 65. Medallion, gold and accents. H & Co. (7).

538. WYE saucer, 5½″ diameter. Blank: *Crow'sfoot.* Backmark: J. Color code: Flowers, 4, 3. Foliage, 27 touched with 4. H & Co. (37).

539. TEXAS BLUE BONNET bone dish, 6¼″ by 3⅞″. Blank: *Marseille*. Backmark: H. Color code: Flowers, 51. Foliage, 27 touched with 13. Shadows, 27. H & Co. (1).

540. SOUNION HEAD cup, 4¾″ diameter. Blank: Lobe at base: *Plain*. Backmark: H. Color code: Flowers, 3, one shade lighter than 4. Scrolls, 18. H & Co. (35).

541. RENDON plate, 9½″ diameter. Blank: *Plain*. Backmark: H. Color code: Flowers, 56, 42, 41, 47. Foliage, 38, 70, three shades lighter than 49. Stems, two shades darker than 69. H & Co. (12).

542. PELOPENNESOS plate, 9¾″ diameter. Blank: *Double Scallops**. Backmark: J. Color code: Foliage and scrolls, 32, three shades lighter than 29, 45, 6. H & Co. (7).

543. ODESSA plate, 9¾″ diameter. Blank: *Plain.* Backmark: J. Color code: Flowers, 4 touched with white. Foliage, 29, 30. Swags, royal purple. H & Co. (13).

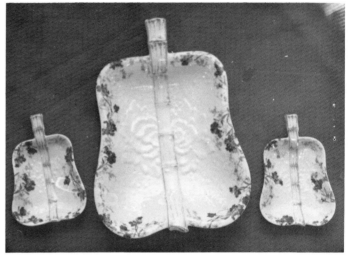

544. NOVEMBER rice set. (Serving dish with twelve individual dishes.) Large dish, 14″. Small dishes, 6½″. Blank: *Fiddle**. Backmark: B. Color code: Foliage, 29 and 30 outlined in 15, 68. Flowers four shades darker than 30, with 6; other flowers, 64, 1, 3. H & Co. (1).

545. MARTIN plate, 9¾″ diameter. Blank: *Plain.* Backmark: J. Color code: Flowers, 1 touched with 2, 27. Foliage, 27, 28, 29. H & Co. (3).

546. UNNAMED saucer, 5³⁄₈″ diameter. Blank: *Plain.* Backmark: J. Color code: Gold only. H & Co. (90).

547. JOSEPHINE TATNALL saucedish, 5⅝″ diameter. Blank: *Plain.* Backmark: J. (Marked Josephine T. on back, but so are others not in any way resembling this.) Color code: Flowers shading from 1 to three shades lighter than 2. Foliage, 29 and one shade lighter. Note: Again the Josephine T. question arises. Readers, please inform me if you know the answer to this. H & Co. (46).

548. FIRST SPRING plate, 8½″ diameter. Blank: *Ranson.* Backmark: H. Color code: Flowers, 8 outlined in 13, 54 with centers of 42. Foliage, 26. Shadows, two shades lighter than 20. H & Co. (1).

549. HENRIETTE saucer, 5⅜″ diameter. Blank: *Ranson.* Backmark: H. Color code: Flowers, 2, 3. Foliage, 19. H & Co. (90).

550. GOLDEN plate, 8⅝″ diameter. Blank: *Diana.* Backmark: J. Color code: Design, 25 with gray added touched with two shades lighter than 13. H & Co. (7).

552. DAWN plate, 9⁷/₈″ diameter. Blank: *Diana*. Color code: Background, 66 at rim shading to almost white with gold enamel. H & Co. (7).

551. ELIZABETH soup tureen lid, 9″ by 11½″. Blank: *Marseille*. Backmark: H. Color code: Flowers, 3, 23. Foliage, two shades darker than 27, 29. Shadows, 68. H & Co. (1).

553. CONDESSA demitasse cup and saucer. Saucer, 4¾″ diameter. Blank: *Vermicelle*. Backmark: B. Color code: Flowers and foliage, eight shades lighter than 30, 16, 69. H & Co. (1).

554. BLUE CARNATIONS soup bowl, 9½″ diameter. Blank: *Marseille*. Backmark: H. Color code: Flowers and foliage, 56 outlined in two shades lighter than 13, one shade lighter than 30. H & Co. (3).

555. ARISTOCRACY plate, 8½″ diameter. Blank: *Pompadour II.* Backmark: I. Color code: Cobalt marli with border of gold leaves and gold snowflakes. Central medallion of antique gold. H & Co. (1).

556. WHITFIELD bowl, 9½″ diameter. Blank: *Bowknots.* Backmark: J. Color code: Flowers, 3, 4, 42, touched with 2. Foliage, 28. Shadows, 50. H & Co. (84).

557. ROWENA tea and toast tray, 8″ long. Blank: *Marseille.* Backmark: H. Color code: Flower centers one shade darker than 60, 67. Foliage, 70, 20 outlined in 14. H & Co. (1).

558. LAKE CHAMPLAIN plate, 8⅝″ diameter. Blank: *Strasburg.* Backmark: J. Color code: Flowers and foliage, 8, 9, 28, 29. H & Co. (40).

559. UNNAMED basket 6³/₈″ long. Blank: *Osier.* Backmark: GG, also English Registry mark incised. Color code: All white. H & Co. (2).

560. ALEUTIAN saucer, 5½″ diameter. Blank: *Silver.* Backmark: J. Color code: Flowers, 6, 5, white, 20. Leaves, 28, 19. H & Co. (17).

561. CLOVER LEAF* butter insert, 4⁵/₈″ diameter. Blank: *Plain.* Backmark: J. Color code: Flowers, 11. Foliage two shades darker than 21. H & Co. (1).

562. SNUG HARBOR cup, 2¹/₈″ diameter. Blank: *Plain.* Backmark: H. Color code: Flowers, 16, two shades darker than 9. Foliage, 21. H & Co. (81).

563. LACE BERTHA plate, 6¼″ diameter. Blank: *Plain.* Backmark: J. Color code: Conventional border two shades darker than 52. Florals, 28. H & Co. (12).

565. SALISBURY saucedish, 5″ diameter. Blank: *Plain.* Backmark: J. Color code: Chain, 38 outlined in one shade darker than 47. Floral links and berries one shade darker than 47. Foliage one shade darker than 40. H & Co. (1).

564. NEW MEXICO SKY petit four, 9″ by 3″ tall. Blank: *Osier.* Backmark: GG. Color code: Flowers, 13, two shades lighter than 13, 6, purple. Foliage two shades lighter than 30, 3, 4, five shades lighter than 36. H & Co. (2).

566. UNNAMED bone dish, 6″ long. Blank: *Crescent Leaf.* Backmark; B. Color code: All white. H & Co. (1).

567. RYAN plate, 9¹¹/₁₆″ diameter. Blank: *Star*. Backmark: J. Color code: Flowers, white touched with 21 and 15; 21 touched with white, 15 and 5; one shade darker than 6 touched with white and 15. Foliage, 20 touched with 15. H & Co. (1).

568. MYCENAE plate, 9¹/₈″ diameter. Blank: *Nenuphar*. Backmark: H. Color code: Design, two shades darker than 19. H & Co. (1).

569. PRIMULAS plate, 7³/₈″ diameter. Blank: *Plain*. Backmark: B. Color code: Flowers, 24, 42 centered with 12, 56. Foliage, 29, 30 touched with enamel. H & Co. (12).

570. MEREDITH cup, 4⁵/₈″ wide by 2¹³/₁₆″ tall. Blank: *Star*. Backmark: J. Color code: Border, three shades darker than 21, gold. Flowers, two shades lighter than 2; 3 touched with 42, 20, 53, two shades lighter than 53. Foliage, 21, three shades lighter than 22. H & Co. (40).

571. MIDSUMMER'S DAY plate, 9½" diameter. Blank: *Plain.* Backmark: J. Color code: Flowers, 3, 4, white. Foliage, 27. H & Co. (56).

572. MONTREAL plate, 8½" diameter. Blank: *Star.* Backmark: J. Color code: Border five shades lighter than 36, 35, one shade darker than 1. Cavetto flowers, 1, 3, 25. Foliage, eight shades lighter than 36; 26 touched with 4. H & Co. (58).

573. END OF SUMMER plate, 8½" diameter. Blank: *Pompadour.* Backmark: B. Color code: Touched with enamel. Flowers, 42, 44, 15. Foliage ten shades lighter than 49, 15. H & Co. (56).

574. DEVON bone dish, 6" long. Blank: *Bowknots*.* Backmark: H. Color code: Flowers, 53, 54, 3 touched with 4. Foliage, 29, 30. H & Co. (28).

575. DARROW saucer, 5½″ diameter. Blank: *Ranson.* Backmark: J. Color code: Flowers two shades lighter than 1; two shades lighter than 42. Stems and centers, 48. Foliage, 27, 28. Shadows, 70, 10. H & Co. (47).

576. DELPHINE plate, 9¾″ diameter. Blank: *Double Scallops*.* Backmark: J. Color code: Flowers, 6, 7, 10, 54. Foliage, 28, 29. H & Co. (40).

577. DROP ROSE** plate, 9⅝″ diameter. Blank: *Star.* Backmark: J. Color code: Flowers, 3, one shade lighter than 3, one shade darker than 4, two shades darker than 4. Foliage, 20, one shade lighter than 20. Note: This also comes in five other colors: blue, green, yellow, lavender and dark red. H & Co. (1).

578. DARTMOUTH cream pitcher, 3⅜″ to lip. Blank: *Diana.* Backmark: B. Color code: Flowers, 23, 24, 42, 47, two shades lighter than 15. Foliage, 15, 16, two shades lighter than 30. H & Co. (1).

579. DIXON pitcher, 10″ in height. Blank: *Pompadour*. Backmark: J. Color code: Conventional border two shades lighter than 30, two shades lighter than 55. H & Co. (27).

581. ST. AUGUSTINE cocoa service. Pot 9⁵/₈″ to lip. Saucer, 4¹/₂″ diameter. Blank: *Double Scallops**. Backmark: J. Color code: Flowers one and three shades darker than 1, 23. Foliage, 21, two shades darker than 21 touched with 24. H & Co. (2).

580. ARNETT saucer, 5³/₈″ diameter. Blank: *Star*. Backmark: J. Color code: Flowers one shade lighter than 6, one and two shades darker than 6, 43, one shade lighter than 43. Stems two shades lighter than 22. H & Co. (81).

582. MAY DAY plate, 9³/₄″ diameter. Blank: *Bowknots**. Backmark: J. Color code: Outside wreath one shade lighter than 53. Swags and medallions, 3, white, one shade lighter than 53. Foliage one shade lighter than 28. H & Co. (52).

584. CARABELLE pedestal cup and saucer. Saucer, 5¼" diameter. Blank: *Plain.* Backmark: J. Color code: Border, 37 with gold leaves and fleurs-de-lys. H & Co. (2).

583. YOSEMITE saucer, 5½" diameter. Blank: *Plain.* Backmark: H. Color code: Border background, 37. Flowers five shades lighter than 15, one shade darker than 3. Small flowers, 42, one shade lighter than 56. Foliage, 20, 21, 18. H & Co. (7).

585. MICHAELANGELO bouillon cup and saucer. Saucer, 5½" diameter. Blank: *Ranson.* Backmark: J. Color code: Cobalt and gold. Note: Also teacup and saucer in this pattern. H & Co. (1).

586. ANGEL FIRE oyster plate, 7¾" diameter. Blank: *Marseille.* Backmark: H. Color code: Flowers and foliage, 37, 42, two shades darker than 9, two shades lighter than 15. Shadow flowers and foliage, 70 and two shades darker than 10. H & Co. (2).

587. BARLEY MILL cup and saucer. Saucer, 5¼″ diameter. Blank: *Diana.* Backmark: B. Color code: Flowers, 8, two shades darker than 8. Foliage, 36, 65. Stems two shades lighter than 13. H & Co. (56).

588. CARNIVAL saucer, 5⅜″ diameter. Blank: *Star.* Backmark: J. Color code: Flowers, 6, 7, one shade darker than 42. Foliage, 20, 21. H & Co. (15).

589. STEVENS dinner plate, 9⅝″ diameter. Blank: *Ranson.* Backmark: J. Color code: Flowers, 1, one, two, and three shades darker than 1. Foliage, 20, 21. Shadows, 70. H & Co. (75).

590. LYTTON plate, 8⁷/₁₆″ diameter. Blank: *Diana.* Backmark: H. Color code: Border flecked with gold and six shades darker than 57. H & Co. (46).

591. VERA CRUZ cup, 3¹/₈″ diameter. Blank: *Diana.* Backmark: H. Color code: Flowers and foliage, 69, 70, 8. H & Co. (56).

592. WINCHESTER bread and butter plate, 6¼″ diameter. Blank: *Ranson.* Backmark: J. Color code: Flowers, 6, 1, 4, 24. Foliage, 28, 29 touched with 4. H & Co. (47).

593. TAMMY saucer, 5³/₈″ diameter. Blank: *Silver.* Backmark: J. Color code: Flowers, 1 touched with 2, 42. Foliage, one shade lighter than 28 touched with 1. Shadows, 63. H & Co. (37).

594. STOCKHOLM demitasse cup and saucer. Saucer, 4³/₈″ diameter. Blank: *Ranson.* Backmark: J. Color code: Flowers, 23, 2, 3. Foliage, 29, 30, 42. Gold filigree ring inside saucer and around cup. H & Co. (2).

595. ROSEDALE luncheon plate, 8⁵/₈″ diameter. Blank: *Silver.*
Backmark: J. Color code: Flowers, 4, 1, white, 48, two shades darker
than 62. Foliage, 28, 29 touched with 4. Shadows, 10. H & Co. (11).

596. PENLEY plate, 9³/₄″ diameter. Blank: *Diana.* Backmark: H.
Color code: Flowers, 1, 2, 3, 65. Foliage, 13, 30. Border and medallion
two shades lighter than 13. H & Co. (2).

597. OCTOBER plate 9½″ diameter. Blank: *Nenuphar.* Backmark:
H. Color code: Flowers, 58, 59, 60. Foliage five shades darker than 45.
H & Co. (65).

598. NARBERTH plate, 9½″ diameter. Blank: *Plain.* Backmark: J.
Color code: Flowers shades of 2 with white, 42 touched with 2, 5; 6
touched with 2 and white. Foliage shades of 21 and 22. H & Co. (12).

599. MOJAVE ROSE plate, 7½″ diameter. Blank: *Plain.* Backmark: J. Color code: Conventional border, interrupted band 43 edged in three shades lighter than 57. Scrolls three shades lighter than 57. Flowers one shade lighter than 12 touched with 41. Foliage, 21, 22. H & Co. (12).

600. KERRY bread and butter plate, 6¼″ diameter. Blank: *Silver.* Backmark: J. Color code: Flowers, 3, 4, white. Foliage one shade lighter than 20, 21, 24. H & Co. (53).

601. ASBURY PARK cup and saucer. Saucer, 4¼″ diameter. Blank: *Diana.* Backmark: B. Color code: Flowers three shades lighter than 61, three shades lighter than 15, 42, three shades lighter than 15. Foliage 67, three shades lighter than 15. H & Co. (2).

602. BEAVER VALLEY saucer, 5³/₈″ diameter. Blank: *Seed Pearls*.* Backmark: J. Color code: Conventional border, 11, 20. Flowers, 3, 4, white, 23. Foliage, 21, 20, 18. H & Co. (40).

263

603. CINDY ramekin, 4½" diameter. Blank: *Silver.* Backmark: J. Color code: Flowers two shades lighter than 2, 6, white. Foliage, 28, white, touched with 3. Shadows, 58 outlined in 6. H & Co. (40).

604. SAUSALITO sugar bowl, cream pitcher, basket. Basket, 5" by 7³/₈". Blank: *Plain.* Backmark: J. Color code: Flowers and foliage, 45, 65, 20, all with gold handles. H & Co. (2).

605. LENOX AUTUMN covered vegetable dish, 10³/₈" by 7½". Blank: *Unknown.* Backmark: H, factory #9791. Color code: Flowers, 9, 12. Foliage, 26, 27. H & Co. (56).

606. UNNAMED toothpick holder, 2¼" tall. Blank: *Marseille.* Backmark: B. Color code: All white. Note: First toothpick holder seen. H & Co. (1).

607. WENDY saucer, 5½" diameter. Blank: *Ranson.* Backmark: J. Color code: Flowers two shades darker than 4, 4, 3. Foliage, 22. H & Co. (37).

608. TRACY dinner plate, 9½" diameter. Blank: *Plain.* Backmark: J. Color code: Flowers, 38, two shades lighter than 38. Foliage, 29 outlined in 13. H & Co. (17).

609. SANDERSON plate, 8⁵/₈″ diameter. Blank: *Plain.* Backmark: J. Color code: Flowers, 4, 23. Foliage, 25. H & Co. (12).

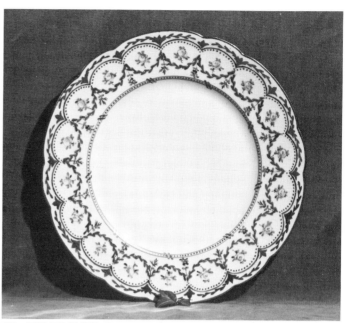

610. RIO GRANDE plate, 8³/₈″ diameter. Blank: *Diana.* Backmark: J. Color code; Conventional border, thin line of 57. Flowers, 4, 3, 1, white, 54, royal purple. Foliage 30. Double band, gold dots, two shades lighter than 57. H & Co. (3).

611. PERSIAN saucer, 5½″ diameter. Blank: *Diana.* Backmark: J. Factory mark: #17225. Feston . . . T . . . K. Color code: Border, elaborate gold design. Flowers, 58, 59, 61, 64. Foliage two shades lighter than 20. Note: This is a sample piece. H & Co. (1).

612. OLYMPIA saucer, 5″ diameter. Blank: *Diana.* Backmark: H. Color code: Greek key, gold. Figures, 64, 65 touched with 2. H & Co. (3).

613. NEW HAVEN platter, 12" x 8½". Blank: *Star.* Backmark: J. Color code: Flowers, 1, and five shades lighter than 2, one shade lighter than 56. Foliage, 20, 21. H & Co. (7).

614. MC NEILL gravy or sauceboat, 2½" to lip. Blank: *Plain.* Backmark: J. Color code: border, 29, 63. Flowers, 4, 3. H & Co. (52).

615. KATHARINE saucer, 5³/₈" diameter. Blank: *Pompadour.* Backmark: J. Color code: Border, gold and four shades darker than 22. Flowers, 1 shading to white. Foliage one shade lighter than 29 shading to four shades lighter than 29. Shadows one shade lighter than 63. H & Co. (15).

616. JACKSON plate, 9½" diameter. Blank: *Ranson.* Backmark: J. Color code: Flowers, 5, 6. Foliage, shades of 28. H & Co. (65).

617. JANET LOUISE plate, 9⅝" diameter. Blank: *Silver.* Backmark: J. Color code: Flowers, 3, 4, white, six shades lighter than 20. Foliage, 22, 27, white, 42 touched with 4. Shadows eight shades lighter than 20 touched with 3. H & Co. (52).

618. HARVEST GLORY sugar bowl, 4½" to top of finial. Blank: *Triangle.* Backmark: B, plus English Registry mark. Color code: One-inch border, 10, with flat braided handles outlined in gold. Flowers four shades lighter than 2, 3, and white. Foliage, 38, 40, 13. H & Co. (2).

619. GLASTONBURY dessert sugar bowl and creamer. Bowl, 3½" tall. Blank: *Ranson.* Backmark: H. Color code: Flowers, 30, 48. Foliage, 30, 48. Trellis two shades darker than 45. Shadows, 58. H & Co. (2).

620. FANTASIA plate, 9" diameter. Blank: *Bowknots*.* Backmark: I. Color code: Flowers, 20, 21 with gold, 70. Foliage, 69, 70. Swirls, 69, 70. Rim background, 36 fading to white. H & Co. (1).

621. ERIN plate, 9⅝" diameter. Blank: *Crow'sfoot**. Backmark: J. Color code: Conventional border, scrolls, 20. Lattice, 20. Flowers, 35. H & Co. (12).

622. DELIGHT cup and saucer. Saucer, 5⅜" diameter. Blank: *Plain.* Backmark: J. Color code: Flowers, 4, 5, 42, three shades darker than 56. Foliage, 20. H & Co. (23).

623. CHO CHO SAN salad plate, 8½" by 5¼". Blank: *Plain.* Backmark: EE. Color code: Flowers, foliage, and characters two shades lighter than 12, 13, 1, two shades lighter than 22, black, 32. This is a salad plate, not a bone dish. The shape and pattern are both rare, particularly the shape for a salad plate. This is a Frank Haviland backmark. Frank Hav. (1).

624. BERMUDA pedestal cocoa cup and saucer. Saucer, 5¼" diameter. Blank: *Smooth.* Backmark: J. Color code: Flowers, 3, 67, 42, 2. Foliage, 29, 37, 42, 2, 67, 65. H & Co. (2).

625. ALONZO punch cup, 3⁷/₈″ diameter. Blank: *Ranson*. Backmark: J. Color code: Flowers, 1 touched with 4, 42 touched with white, 65. Foliage, shades of 68, 36 touched with 4. H & Co. (1).

626. SHELBY demitasse cup and saucer. Saucer, 4¼″ diameter. Blank: *Cannelé*. Backmark: I. Color code: Flowers and foliage, 68, 69, 2, 5. Colors are the same but florals differ on various pieces and blanks. H & Co. (2).

627. CHANTILLY* saucer, 5¼″ diameter. Blank: *Ranson*. Backmark: J. Color code: Flowers and foliage five shades lighter than 2, 37. H & Co. (6).

628. WATCH HILL individual cocoa pot, 5″ to lip. Blank: *Double Scallops*. Backmark: J. Color code: Flowers, 2, 3, 67. Foliage, 20, 21 outlined in 2. H & Co. (2).

629. OCTAVIA demitasse cup and saucer. Saucer, 4¼″ diameter. Blank: *Unknown.* Backmark: I. Color code: Flowers, 23, white, 15, 36, 14, all outlined in 15. H & Co. (2).

631. HALIBURTON bread and butter plate, 6¼″ diameter. Blank: *Plain.* Backmark: J. Color code: Conventional border two shades darker than 57 with diamonds of 43. Flowers one shade lighter than 13, 45. Foliage three shades lighter than 36, 38, 57. Stems one shade lighter than 13. H & Co. (87).

630. CLIMBING ROSE dinner plate, 9½″ diameter. Blank: *Diana.* Backmark: H. Color code: Flowers, 3, 23. Foliage two shades lighter than 18. Lattice, 68. H & Co. (1).

632. SUTTON PLACE pitcher, 3¼″ to tip of spout. Blank: *Marseille.* Backmark: H. Color code: Design two shades darker than 50, gold encrusted. H & Co. (7).

270

633. LAURA plate, 8½" diameter. Blank: *Ranson.* Backmark: J. Color code: Flowers, 7, 23, 5, white. Foliage, 28. Shadows one shade lighter than 68. H & Co. (7).

634. ROSETTA plate, 9¾" diameter. Blank: *Double Scallops.* Backmark: J. Color code: Flowers, 9, 27. Foliage, 22. Shadow, 9. H & Co. (52).

635. LETITIA saucer, 5½" diameter. Blank: *Star.* Backmark: J. Color code: Flowers, 4, 3, white, 32, 34. Foliage, 21, two shades darker than 21. H & Co. (12).

636. NARAGANSETT plate, 9¾" diameter. Blank: *Diana.* Backmark: B. Color code: Flowers, 4 outlined in 13. Foliage, 32, three shades lighter than 36 streaked with 32 and white. Medallion, gold. H & Co. (7).

637. LA LUZ saucer, 5¼" diameter. Blank: *Star*. Backmark: J. Color code: Flowers four shades lighter than 11, two shades darker than 34. Foliage two shades darker and one shade lighter than 21. H & Co. (81).

638. FIELD FLOWERS covered bowl, 6" by 6" by 2½" tall. Blank: *Cannelé*. Backmark: B. Color code: Flowers, 42, 30, 25, 64, 47. Foliage, 69, 25. H & Co. (2).

639. CHERRY HILL cup and saucer. Saucer, 4³/₈" diameter. Blank: *Diana*. Backmark: B. Color code: Flowers two shades lighter than 1; centers, 55, 16. Stems, 14. Foliage, 42, 52. H & Co. (46).

640A. COIMBRA covered vegetable dish also in *Star* blank.

640. COIMBRA luncheon plate, 8½" diameter. Blank: *Star*. Backmark: J. Factory #17889. Color code: Flowers and foliage, 66, 64, 42, 4, 5, 48, 56, two shades lighter than 39, 13, 68, 10. H & Co. (66).

642. CARLSBAD plate, 9⅝″ diameter. Blank: *Strasburg.* Backmark: B. Color code: Flowers, 4, 5, 56. Foliage ten shades lighter than 14. H & Co. (15).

641. CHARYBDIS demitasse cup and saucer. Saucer, 4¼″ diameter. Blank; *Plain.* Backmark: K. Color code: Background, 36 with gold. Flowers, 23, 3, 65, white enamel. Foliage, 20, 21, 65. H & Co. (2).

643. CHARMER saucer, 5⅝″ diameter. Blank: *Plain.* Backmark: E. Color code: Leaves, 15, 16, touched with 65, 30. H & Co. (3).

644. CHATHAM plate, 8½″ diameter. Blank: *Crow'sfoot*.* Backmark: J, Factory #15578. Color code: Flowers and foliage, 6, 7, one shade lighter than 6, one shade lighter than 28, 25, 5. H & Co. (66).

273

645. DYNASTY cup and saucer. Cup, 3⁵/₈″, Saucer, 5⁷/₁₆″. Blank: *Plain*. Backmark: J. Color code: Border, gold and cobalt. Flowers, 3, and blends of lighter shades of 3. Foliage, 21. H & Co. (46).

647. MAYWOOD ramekin and saucer. Ramekin, 3½″ diameter. Saucer, 5¼″ diameter. Blank: *Plain*. Backmark: J. Color code: Flowers, 6, 7. Foliage, 28, 21. Note: Maywood was the name of the family home of the Mayo family of Rochester, Minnesota, clinic fame. The pattern belonged to Mrs. Charles Mayo who sold it for a youth center benefit in Rochester. H & Co. (30).

646. SWEET BRIAR plate, 8⁵/₈″ diameter. Blank: *Ranson*. Backmark: J. Color code: Flowers, 2, 6, 3, 42. Foliage, 36, 19. Shadows two shades lighter than 70. (Touched with enamel.) H & Co. (1).

648. YORKLYN six-cup tray, 17¾″ long. Blank: *Unknown*. Backmark: J. Color code: Border, 27, 36. Flowers, 3, and 6 blending to white with centers of 20. Foliage, 20, 21 outlined with 62. H & Co. (2).

649. COREOPSIS covered gravy boat on tray, 8¾″ by 5¼″. Blank: *Ranson.* Backmark: H. Color code: Flowers, 42, 43, two shades lighter than 13. Foliage, 48, 27, two shades lighter than 13. H & Co. (56).

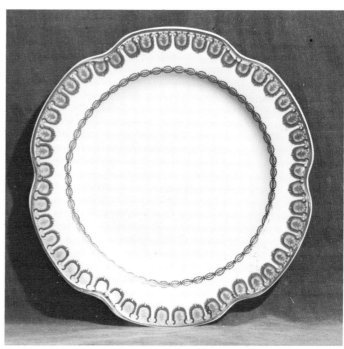

650. MONTERREY plate, 6¼″ diameter. Blank: *Silver.* Backmark: J. Color code: Conventional border, 30 and gold. H & Co. (12).

651. HUSBANDS plate, 9½″ diameter. Blank: *Silver.* Backmark: J. Color code: Flowers and foliage, 27, one shade lighter than 20 outlined in 16. Note: This is really a surname. H & Co. (52).

652. GLACIER LAKE cup and saucer. Saucer, 4¼″ diameter. Blank: *Pompadour.* Backmark: B. A la Paix, J. Mabot, 34 Avenue de l'Opera, Paris. Color code: Flowers, 2, 62, white outlined in one shade lighter than 15. Foliage one shade lighter than 15, 30 touched with 2. H & Co. (2).

653. FLAMENCO plate, 8½" diameter. Blank: *Cannelé*. Backmark: B. Color code: Marli, 59. Cavetto: Flowers, 65, 2, 6, 42. Foliage two shades darker than 21, 70. H & Co. (1).

654. ELLIS saucer, 5½" diameter. Blank: *Plain*. Backmark: J. Color code: Flowers, 3, 4. Foliage, 21. H & Co. (1).

655. DIERKES teacup and saucer. Saucer, 5¼" diameter. Blank: *Star*. Backmark: J. Color code: Flowers, 4, one shade darker than 4. Foliage, one shade lighter than 29, 28 touched with 4. H & Co. (84).

656. CHISHOLM soup bowl, 9⅛" diameter. Blank: *Star*. Backmark: J. Color code: Conventional border, 47, two shades lighter than 36. H & Co. (53).

657. BRECKENRIDGE plate, 8½″ diameter. Blank: *Plain.* Backmark: J. Factory #16348 in red, followed by Josephine . . . T . . . L. Color code: Border two shades lighter than 36, gold dots and foliate wreath. Similar narrow inner border. Gold medallion in center. Josephine is a confusing factory addition. If anyone knows why "Josephine," with letters after the name, should appear on several different patterns, please send me the information for inclusion in the first supplement. H & Co. (54).

658. APOLLO cup and saucer. Saucer, 5⅛″ diameter. Blank: *Bowknots*.* Backmark: H. Color code: Flowers, 56. Foliage, 18. Border, gold swirls on 49. H & Co. (65).

659. STOCKDALE plate, 9⅝″ diameter. Blank: *Star.* Backmark: D. Color code: Flowers, 2, 3, 6. Foliage two shades lighter than 22. H & Co. (1).

660. SAVANNAH bowl, 5″ diameter. Blank: *Plain.* Backmark: J. Color code: Conventional border, gold, black, 6, 53, 43. Custom-made piece with decorator's mark in gold. H & Co. (28).

661. SPRING TRIUMPH saucer, 5½" diameter. Blank: *Ranson.*
Backmark: J. Color code: Flowers, 7, two shades lighter than 7, two
shades darker than 7, 41; 35, one shade darker, one shade lighter than
35. Foliage two shades darker than 21. H & Co. (81).

662. STORRS saucer, 5³/8" diameter. Blank: *Silver.* Backmark: J.
Color code: Flowers, 3, 4, 5. Foliage, 24, 27. Shadows, 23. H & Co.
(40).

663. CHAPIN plate, 8³/8" diameter. Blank: *Diana.* Backmark: H.
Color code: Flowers, 6, 5. Stems four shades lighter than 13. Foliage,
25. Shadows, 70. H & Co. (40).

664. MARY HELEN saucedish, 5⁵/16" diameter. Blank: *Pompadour.*
Backmark: B. Color code: Flowers, 42, 69, one shade lighter than 65.
Foliage, 3. H & Co. (37).

278

665. EMBASSY* bread and butter plate, 6½" diameter. Blank: *Wheat.* Backmark: RR. Color code: White with gold band toward inner rim. Amer. Theo (1).

666. UNNAMED covered vegetable dish, 7" to top of finial. Blank: *Sèvres.* Backmark: A. Color code: Gold only. H & Co. (29).

667. DALMATIA bonbon dish, 6¾" by 5¾". Blank: *Ranson.* Backmark: J. Color code: Border scroll, flowers, foliage, 20 touched with 13. Shadow, 62. Flowers, shades darker than lighter than 5 touched with 42. Foliage, 21 touched with 42, 13. H & Co. (1).

668. BIT O'SKY saucer, 5³⁄₈" diameter. Blank: *Ranson.* Backmark: H. Color code: Flowers, 51, 52. Foliage, 27, 28 touched with 15. H & Co. (15).

669. ALAN chocolate pot, 7½" tall. Blank: *Nenuphar Plain.* Backmark: J. Color code: Stripes one shade darker than 64. Flowers, 64, 23, white. Foliage, 20, 21. H & Co. (1).

670. PARAMOUNT* plate, 8" diameter. Blank: *Plain.* Backmark: X. Color code: Border one shade lighter than 22, white, four shades darker than 1, edged in black. Flowers four shades darker than 1, 53, 55, 45, 42, white, 41. H & Co. (12).

671. PAGODAS plate, 9⅝" diameter. Blank: *Diana.* Backmark: H. Color code: Border two shades darker than 24. Flowers, 1, three shades darker than 1. Trellis and foliage, 70. H & Co. (6).

672. NORMAN plate, 7⅝" diameter. Blank: *Marseille.* Backmark: B. Color code: Flowers, 1, one shade darker than 1 tipped with one shade darker than 52. Foliage, 30, one shade lighter and one shade darker than 30. H & Co. (46).

674. SPRINGHILL saucer, 5³/₈″ diameter. Blank: *Ranson.* Backmark: J. Color code: Flowers, 11, 3. Foliage, 28. H & Co. (90).

673. SICILY plate, 6¹/₈″ diameter. Blank: *Strasburg.* Backmark: J. Color code: Flowers, 3, 4. Foliage, 27 touched with 4, 26. H & Co. (35).

675. CELTIC cup, 3½″ by 2″. Blank: *Plain.* Backmark: J. Color code: Conventional border. Flowers, 4 touched with 12. Foliage, 40 touched with 12. H & Co. (56).

676. STACY dessert plate, 7½″ diameter. Blank: *Plain.* Backmark: J. Color code: Flowers, 13. Foliage, 13 and 40. Border, gold. H & Co. (28).

677. LOUISE short cocoa cup and saucer. Saucer, 4⁷/₈″ diameter. Blank: *Ranson*. Backmark: H. Color code: Flowers, 3, 5, touched with 2. Foliage, 20 touched with 2. Scrolls, 42 touched with 2. H & Co. (2).

678. VALLE GRANDE plate, 9½″ diameter. Blank: *Diana*. Backmark: B. Color code: Flowers three shades darker than 46 outlined in 47, 63. Foliage, 70. Shadows, 36 outlined in two shades darker than 36. H & Co. (7).

679. WINNIE FAY saucer, 5³/₈″ diameter. Blank: *Ranson*. Backmark: H. Color code: Flowers, 62, 4. Foliage one shade lighter than 28. H & Co. (90).

680. TAFT tea and toast cup and tray. Cup, 3³/₈″ in diameter, 2¹/₈″ tall. Blank: *Ranson*. Backmark: B. Color code: Flowers, 58, 59, 60. Foliage, 69, 70, 9 and one shade lighter than 9. Ribbon, 69. H & Co. (1).

681. SUMMER SUNSHINE plate, 7½″ diameter. Blank: *Plain.* Backmark: J. Color code: Flowers, 42. Foliage, 25. H & Co. (3).

682. RENAISSANCE dinner plate, 9½″ diameter. Blank: *Plain.* Backmark: J. Color code: Conventional border two shades lighter than 57, two shades lighter than 22; 5, white. H & Co. (17).

683. PARISIEN* saucer, 5³⁄₈″ diameter. Blank: *Plain.* Backmark: J. Color code: Band one shade lighter than 23. Rim, gold. Baskets in center, 14, white. Foliage, 57, 14. Chain, 57, 14. H & Co. (1).

684. O'FLAHERTY saucer, 6″ diameter. Blank: *Ormolu Buckles*.* Backmark: J. Color code: Flowers, 1, white, 24 touched with three shades lighter than 13. Foliage, 21, one shade darker than 21. H & Co. (28).

685. NORTH DAKOTA WHEAT plate, 10″ diameter. Blank: *Silver.* Backmark: J. Color code: Flowers and foliage, 5, 26, 32. H & Co. (28).

686. MORTON dinner plate, 9½″ diameter. Blank: *Plain.* Backmark: J. Color code: Conventional border, 28, 13, 6, two shades lighter than 37. H & Co. (17).

687. LEIGH six-cup tray, 17½″ by 18″. Blank: *Ranson.* Backmark: J. Color code: Border three shades darker than 38. Flowers, 4, 5, 61 blending to white. Foliage one shade darker than 18, 20, 21 outlined with 62 touched with 3. H & Co. (2).

688. JUNE pitcher, 8″ tall. Blank: *Ranson.* Backmark: J. Color code: Flowers one and two shades darker than 1, 23, 68, touched with enamel. Foliage, 27, two shades darker than 27, two shades lighter than 36. H & Co. (1).

689. HARRIET saucer, 5½″ diameter. Blank: *Diana.* Backmark: J. Color code: Flowers, 3 shading to white, touched with 4. Foliage, 20, 21. H & Co. (15).

690. GOLDEN TAB saucer, 4⅝″ diameter. Blank: *Plain.* Backmark: J. Color code: Conventional border in gold on 36. H & Co. (1).

691. FRONTENAC* saucer, 5⅜″ diameter. Blank: *Ranson.* Backmark: J. Color code: Flowers, 6, 5 fading to white touched with 70. Foliage, 29 shading to ten shades lighter. H & Co. (29).

692. EVELYN saucer, 5⅜″ diameter. Blank: *Silver.* Backmark: J. Color code: Flowers one shade lighter than 4, white tipped with 15, two shades darker than 25. Stems and foliage, 35 tipped with 42. H & Co. (15).

693. DALHOUSIE punch cup, 3⁷/₈" by 3". Blank: *Ranson.* Backmark: J. Color code: Flowers, 5, 11, 65, 66, touches of 13 and gold. Foliage, 5, 27, 28 outlined in 15. H & Co. (1).

694. CARTER saucer, 4½" diameter. Blank: *Bowknots*.* Backmark: J. Color code: Flowers, 6 touched with 23, white. Centers touched with 2. Foliage two shades darker than 18 touched with 2. Stems, 2. Shadows one shade lighter than 20. H & Co. (1).

695. THE BRETAGNE* plate, 7³/₈" diameter. Blank: *Ranson.* Backmark: J. Color code: Flowers, 31, white; some flowers and buds outlined in two shades darker than 45. Foliage, 20, 3. Stems outlined in two shades darker than 45. Shadows same as foliage. H & Co. (1).

696. ARCADY saucer, 4¼" diameter. Blank: *Ranson.* Backmark: B. Color code: Flowers, 6 touched with white enamel. Foliage, 22, 23 touched with 1. Shadows, 68. H & Co. (65).

697. CHICAGO saucer, 5¾" diameter. Blank: *Plain.* Backmark: J. Color code: Conventional border background, 24; wreath in three shades lighter than 57. Flowers, 5 touched with 2, 19. Foliage, 29, 27. H & Co. (15).

698. MADAME POMPADOUR saucer, 5⅝" diameter. Blank: *Diana.* Backmark: H. Color code: Flowers, 65, 66. Foliage, 20. Cavetto in Madame Pompadour rose. H & Co. (6).

699. AGAMEMNON demitasse cup and saucer. Saucer, 4½" diameter. Blank: *Double Scallops.* * Backmark: J. Color code: Flowers, 5, gold, four shades darker than 20, white outlined with 2. Foliage four shades darker than 20 outlined in 2. H & Co. (2).

700. LEVERETT saucer, 5⅜" diameter. Blank: *Plain.* Backmark: J. Color code: Conventional border, 37, one shade lighter than 15, one shade darker than 42. Flowers, 2, 23, 3. Foliage, 21, 25 touched with 6. H & Co. (17).

701. GIRARD'S CROSS saucer, 5³/₈″ diameter. Blank: *Ranson.* Backmark: J. Color code: Flowers two shades darker than 52, 5, 63, 50. Foliage, 29, 28. H & Co. (17).

702. KUNGSHOLM cup and saucer, five o'clock size. Blank: *Ranson.* Backmark: J, Feu de Four. Color code: Allover pattern, 67, 68, 69 blended to two shades lighter than 37. H & Co. (2).

703. CHENAULT cup and saucer. Saucer, 4⁵/₈″ diameter. Blank: *Bowknots**. Backmark: J. Color code: Flowers two shades lighter than 2, three shades lighter than 15, 58, 62. Foliage, 20. H & Co. (70).

704. UNNAMED pot de creme. Saucer, 4³/₄″ diameter. Blank: *Ruby.* Backmark: B. Color code: Gold banding only. Cup is twelve-sided. This is an extremely early pattern and style. H & Co. (10).

705. VAN NOSTRAND plate, 9¾″ diameter. Blank: *Ranson.* Backmark: J, Factory #22903. Color code: Flowers, 4, 3. Foliage, 31, 30. H & Co. (7).

706A. LATE FALL vegetable bowl, side view.

708. PANSIES saucer, 5¼″ diameter. Blank: *Diana.* Backmark: H. Color code: Flowers, 60, two shades darker than 62, white, touched with 14. Foliage two shades lighter than 22. H & Co. (56).

706. LATE FALL vegetable bowl, 10⅛″ by 6⅜″. Blank: *Crescent.* Backmark: B. Color code: Flowers and foliage, 15, 12, 10, five shades lighter than 15, 63, 21, 30, 14. Daubed with gold. H & Co. (29).

707. BERKELEY* plate 6⅜″ diameter. Blank: *Plain.* Backmark: TT. Color code: One broad and two narrow bands of gold. Note: This is an exception to the rule of not naming patterns with gold decoration only, but the exception was made at the factory, not by this author. Amer. Haviland (9).

710. LEESBURG butter pat, 3″ diameter. Blank: *Ranson.* Backmark: J. Color code: Flowers, 4, white, two shades lighter than 1. Foliage and stems, 2, 22. Shadows one shade lighter than 68. H & Co. (74).

709. IRISH CARAVANS saucer, 5³/₈″ diameter. Blank: *Star.* Backmark: J. Color code: Flowers, 3, 23, white, 34, 35. Foliage, 21, 20, 34, touched with three shades lighter than 15. H & Co. (60).

711. PRUDENCE oval dish, 5″ by 6″. Blank: *Unknown.* Backmark: X. Color code: Flowers, 3, 4, white. Foliage two shades darker than 21. H & Co. (79).

712. DVORAK saucedish, 5³/₄″ diameter. Blank: *Strasburg.* Backmark: H. Color code: Flowers two shades lighter than 13, white, 70, 45, 5. Grasses, 21, 43. H & Co. (79).

713. CATHEDRAL CLOSE dinner plate, 9¼″ diameter. Blank: *Star.*
Backmark: J. Color code: Flowers, 1, 5, two shades lighter than 2, 42,
white, two shades lighter than 57. Foliage, 22, white, 20, 18 touched
with 13, 14, 3, 42, 2. Shadows, 23, 67. H & Co. (33).

714. SPRING MORNING demitasse cup and saucer. Saucer, 4½″
diameter. Blank: *Plain.* Backmark: J. Color code: Flowers, 65, 66,
15, two shades darker than 42, 32, 15, all outlined in gold. Foliage, 25,
15 outlined in gold, 12, 62, 53. H & Co. (2).

715. LUCY demitasse cup and saucer. Saucer, 4¼″ diameter. Blank:
Marseille. Backmark: H. Color code: Design, 53, 63. H & Co. (2).

716. THE VINCENNES* bread and butter plate, 6⅛″ diameter. Blank:
Plain. Backmark: J. Color code: Flowers, 56, two shades darker than
56, 43, 52, white. Beads, 43. Scrolls, 43. Band two shades darker than
56. Rim, gold. H & Co. (1).

717. WESTOVER plate, 9¾" diameter. Blank: *Double Scallops**. Backmark: J, Factory #22655. Color code: Flowers, white tipped with 3, 64, 41. Foliage two shades lighter than 28 tipped with 6. H & Co. (6).

718. TRUMPETER SWAN saucer, 5¼" diameter. Blank: *Plain*. Backmark: J. Color code: Flowers, 1, 2. Foliage, 29, 27. H & Co. (12).

719. SHAMROCK plate, 9⅝" diameter. Blank: *Plain*. Backmark: J. Color code: Conventional border, 29 outlined in 13. H & Co. (12).

720. ROBERTSON cocoa cup saucer, 5" diameter. Blank: *Silver*. Backmark: J. Color code: Flowers, 3, 4, 59 all touched with white. Foliage, 27 touched with 3. H & Co. (65).

721. PRINCESS* plate, 9⁵/₈" diameter. Blank: *Silver.* Backmark: J. Color code: Flowers, 1, white. Foliage, 27. Stems, 40. Scrolls, 36. Another type of PRINCESS on a different blank. H & Co. (52).

722. O'REILLEY saucer, 5³/₈" diameter. Blank: *Plain.* Backmark: J. Color code: Border, 47, 29, 39. Foliage and flowers, 34, 35, 20, 21 touched with 13. H & Co. (1).

723. NATCHEZ bowl, 5" diameter. Blank: *Plain.* Backmark: J. Color code: Conventional border, gold trim with satin and mirror finish. Custom-made with gold decorator's mark. H & Co. (28).

724. MARGARET POWERS cocoa cup and saucer. Saucer, 5¹/₈" diameter. Blank: *Ranson.* Backmark: J. Color code: Flowers, 3, 63, 56, 42. Foliage, 28 touched with 15. H & Co. (38).

725. TRESSE plate, 8" diameter. Blank: *Osier*. Backmark: B. Color code: Enameled foliage, 22, 61, 62, 14, 15, 68, 69, 20. Shells, 14, 69, 70, 24, 32, 20, 42. Fish, 23, 69, 70, 14. H & Co. (2).

726. LAN SING butter pat, 2⅝" diameter. Blank: *Plain*. Backmark: B. Color code: Flowers and foliage, 53, 42, 68, 69, 70. H & Co. (1).

727. JUNIPER plate, 8¼" diameter. Blank: *Pompadour*. Backmark: B. Color code: Flowers two shades darker than 60, two shades lighter than 61. Foliage 20, 21. H & Co. (12).

728. HALLORAN saucer, 6" diameter. Blank: *Crow'sfoot** Backmark: J. Color code: Wreath, 28, three shades deeper than 31. H & Co. (12).

729. GOLDEN LACE plate, 9¼" diameter. Blank: *Diana.* Backmark: H. Color code: Background four shades darker than 28, 2. Edging, gold. H & Co. (7).

730. ELLSWORTH salad plate, 7½" diameter. Blank: *Star.* Backmark: J. Color code: Flowers, 50, 2, white. Foliage, 22, 48. H & Co. (17).

731. UNNAMED saucer, 5½" diameter. Blank: *Diana.* Backmark: H. Color code: Gold, only. H & Co. (15).

732. FLOWERING FIELDS plate, 8¼" diameter. Blank: *Pompadour.* Backmark: B. Color code: Flowers, 9, one shade lighter than 13. Tiny flowers and grasses, 56, 42. H & Co. (12).

734. SANTA ANA plate, 8⅝″ diameter. Blank: *Plain.* Backmark: J. Color code: Flowers, 4, 5, white outlined in 4. Foliage, 27, white touched with 5. H & Co. (28).

733. DURHAM plate, 9⅝″ diameter. Blank: *Plain.* Backmark: J. Color code: Flowers, 4, 7, 59. Foliage, 28, 29 touched with 5. H & Co. (16).

735. LONGWOOD cup and saucer. Cup, 3½″ by 1⅞″. Saucer, 5⅜″. Blank: *Plain.* Backmark: J, Factory #23359. Color code: Conventional border, gold on cobalt. H & Co. (46).

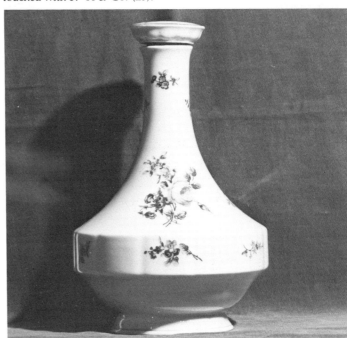

736. CHANTILLY* liquor decanter, 8½″ tall. Blank: *Plain.* Backmark: J. Color code: Large flowers, 2 touched with white; two shades darker than 2 touched with 59, with 24 centers. Small flowers, 15 touched with 24 and black; 59 touched with 2; 42 touched with black; three shades darker than 66 touched with 59. Foliage two shades lighter than 30; 23 touched with black and 13. H & Co. (1).

737. WHITFORD egg cup. Top, 2½"; bottom, 2" diameter. Blank: *Plain.* Backmark: QQ. Color code: Flowers and foliage, 5, 6, one shade darker than 41, two shades lighter than 2. Shadows, 41. H & Co. (54).

739. CHIPPENHAM cup. Blank: *Bowknots**. Backmark: J. Color code: Scrolls, 70 outlined in 15. Flowers one shade lighter than 61, three shades lighter than 3, two shades lighter than 42. Foliage two shades lighter than 26, one shade lighter than 70 outlined in 15. H & Co. (50).

738. PERSEPHONE relish dish, 14" by 7¼". Blank: *Silver.* Backmark: J. Color code: Flowers, 5, 6, 65. Foliage, 22, two shades lighter than 22 touched with 2. Shadows, 25, 23. H & Co. (36).

740. PASSION FLOWERS cocoa pot, 8½" to spout. Blank: *Pompadour.* Backmark: HH. Color code: Flowers, 2, 61. Foliage one shade darker than 30, three shades lighter than 22. H & Co. (29).

741. MALIGNES luncheon plate, 8½″ diameter. Blank: *Diana.* Backmark: FF. Color code: Conventional border, 11, three shades lighter than 36 with gold. Flowers, 61, 70. H & Co. (7).

742. GRANDEUR tureen underplate, 13″ diameter. Blank: *Diana.* Backmark: C. Color code: Border two shades lighter than 2, one shade darker than 33 and gold. H & Co. (2).

Theodore Haviland Patterns

743. UNNAMED plate, 9″ diameter. Blank: *St. Cloud.* Backmark: U, factory artist, J. Martin. Color code: Border, 55, gold floral. Background, 69, 70, 10. Fowl, 68, 69, 48, 49, 15. Flowers, 61, 62. Foliage, 9, 20, 26. Theo. (2).

744. UNNAMED game platter, 13½″ by 18½″. Blank: *St. Cloud.* Backmark: U, factory artist, J. Martin. Color code: Border, 55, gold floral. Water, 67, 64, 65 touched with white enamel. Sky, white, 9, 64. Fowl, 6, 20, 49, 30, 67, 69, 62, 42. Theo. (2).

746. PEINTURE plate, 10″ diameter. Blank: *Louis XV.* Backmark: R. Color code: Flowers one shade lighter than 2, 3, 23. Foliage two shades lighter than 29. Shadows two shades lighter than 32. Theo (41).

745. EDGEWOOD plate, 6⅝″ diameter. Blank: *Plain.* Backmark: JJ. Color code: Flowers, 20 and white, 5 and white, and two shades lighter than 56. Foliage, 20 and white. Stems, 20. Theo (17).

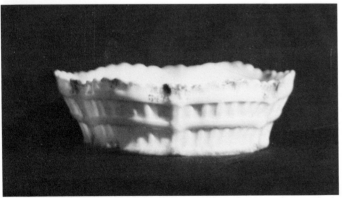

747. UNNAMED hexagonal basket, 5″ to the side, 1¾″ deep. Blank: *Unknown.* Backmark: G. Color code: White and gold. Theo (2).

748. UNNAMED cocoa pot, 8½″ to lip. Blank: *Boucher.* Backmark: S. Color code: All gold trim and gold encrusted. This is a cocoa pot rather than coffeepot. Theo (2).

749. UNNAMED plate, 5¾" diameter. Blank: *Alternate Scallops.* *
Backmark: S. Color code: Gold trim. Theo (54).

750. DRYDEN saucer, 5½" diameter. Blank: *Louis XV.* Backmark:
S. Color code: Flowers three shades lighter than 64, 48, white, 15. Foliage three shades lighter than 40, 15, 34. Theo (1).

751. UNNAMED plate, 9¼" diameter. Blank: *Swanson.* Backmark:
Q. Color code: All gold. Theo (12).

752. VARENNE* luncheon plate, 8¾" diameter. Blank: *St. Germain.* Backmark: TT. Color code: Flowers, 4, 6 touched with 2 and white. Foliage, 20 touched with 2. Stems, 2. Theo (1).

753. MONTREUX* plate, 9¾" diameter. Blank: *Pilgrim.* Backmark: U. Color code: Marli background two shades lighter than 23. Band, 42, two shades lighter than 57 outlined in black. Flowers two shades lighter than 57 with centers of 42; 47 with centers of 42; two shades darker than 42 with centers of 47. Foliage, 22, 31. Stems two shades darker than 48. Basket, 57, two shades lighter than 57 and 14. Theo (56).

754. EDITHA saucer, 5¾" diameter. Blank: *Plain.* Backmark: R. Color code: Narrow black and white conventional border. Oval cartouches interspersed with rectangular cartouches. Green background. Foliage, 4, 5, two shades lighter than 2. Banding two shades darker than 43. Theo (43).

755. MANITOU SPRINGS saucer, 5⅝" diameter. Blank: *Louis XV.* Backmark: S. Color code: Flowers, 6, white, 60 touched with 11, 3, 42, 9. Foliage, 26, 29. Shadows, 67. Theo (1).

756. RADFORD cup and saucer. Saucer, 6¼" diameter. Blank: *Geisha.* Backmark: S. Color code: Conventional border, 22, gold. Theo (56).

757. REFLECTIONS saucer, 5³/₈″ diameter. Blank: *Theo Haviland Ranson.* Backmark: II. Color code: Flowers, 5, 42, 69, 59. Shadows two shades lighter than 34. This pattern can be found on a plain blank, also. Theo (81).

758. YVONNE saucer, 5⁵/₈″ diameter. Blank: *Triple Ripple**. Backmark: R. Color code: Flowers, 3, 4, two shades lighter than 2. Foliage, 28, 27, 29. Theo (47).

759. UNNAMED saucer, 5¹/₂″ diameter. Blank: *Plain.* Backmark: JJ. Color code: Gold trim. Theo (63).

760. MONT MERY* teapot, 5⁵/₈″ diameter. Blank: *Unknown.* Backmark: T. Color code: Flowers four shades lighter than 57. Foliage, 31, 30. Theo (77).

303

761. KEY LARGO tea set. Tray, 17½″ diameter. Teapot, 4¼″ to tip of spout. Cream pitcher, 3¾″ to tip of spout. Sugar bowl, 4½″ to tip of finial. Saucer, 4½″ diameter. Blank: *Theo Haviland Ranson.* Backmark: Q. Color code: Flowers, 32, 64, 70. Centers, 42, 15. Foliage two shades lighter than 29, 70. Theo (2).

763. REPULSE BAY bouillon cup, 3½″ diameter by 2″. Blank: *Plain.* Backmark: R. Color code: Conventional border, black with tiny design in white. Scrolls, 66. Background one shade lighter than 29. Flowers, 7, 6, 5. Foliage, 20. Theo (19).

762. ICELANDIC bouillon cup, 3⁵⁄₈″ diameter. Blank: *Plain.* Backmark: R. Color code: Conventional border, narrow band of 45, two shades darker than 40, black. Flowers, 3, 1. Foliage, 40. Theo (19).

764. NOSEGAY* plate, 7½″ diameter. Blank: *Pilgrim.* Backmark: U. Color code: Gold-banded marli with entire marli background in one shade lighter than 23 edged with a black line. Flowers, 3, white, two shades lighter than 2, one shade lighter than 23, two shades darker than 66, white, with centers one shade lighter than 45; two shades lighter than 45, white, two shades lighter than 47, 46, one shade lighter than 29, 65, 61, white. Foliage: two shades lighter than 22, 20 touched with 30. Theo (68).

765. UNNAMED soup bowl, 7³/₈″ diameter. Blank: *St. Germain.* Backmark: R. Color code: Gold only. Theo (73).

766. HARRISON ROSE** plate, 8¹³/₁₆″ diameter. Blank: *Louis XV.* Backmark: R. Color code: Flowers, 3, 5, 6, white, 42; centers, 2. Foliage one shade darker than 21 touched with 16. Shadows, 32. Theo (1).

767. HOZU RAPIDS, plate, 9⁵/₈″ diameter. Blank: *Plain.* Backmark: S. Color code: Conventional border bamboo, 25. Flowers, 12, three shades lighter than 12. Pine needles three shades lighter than 36. Foliage two shades lighter than 35, 25. Fruit, 13. Theo (56).

768. FINCHLEY plate, 6⁵/₈″ diameter. Blank: *Marie Antoinette.* Backmark: JJ. Color code: Flowers, 6, 20, 19, white. Foliage, 6, 20. Theo (17).

769. BRIGHAM saucer, 5³/₈" diameter. Blank: *Pilgrim.* Backmark: U. Color code: Conventional border, gold rim. Background, 45. Flowers, fruit, and branches, 70 and black. Theo (17).

770. KNIGHTSBRIDGE plate, 9⁵/₈" diameter. Blank: *St. Germain.* Backmark: JJ. Color code: Flowers, 2, one shade darker than 3, white. Foliage, 20, 21, 32 touched with two shades lighter than 2. Theo (17).

771. MAY QUEEN plate, 6⁵/₈" diameter. Blank: *Romeo.* Backmark: R. Color code: Flowers, 4 shading to white. Foliage, 20, two shades lighter than 22. Theo (7).

772. NEWARK saucer, 5³/₈" diameter. Blank: *Plain.* Backmark: S. Color code: Flowers, 5, 6 with outlining in three shades lighter than 13. Foliage, 28 and two shades lighter than 28. Shadows, 70. Theo (17).

773. NORTHFIELD saucer, 5¾" diameter. Blank: *Pilgrim.* Backmark: U. Color code: Flowers, 13, white, two shades lighter than 57, 25, two shades darker than 48. Stems, 60. Foliage, 22, one shade lighter than 22. Theo (40).

774. NOLAND saucer, 5¾" diameter. Blank: *Pilgrim.* Backmark: U. Color code: Conventional border one shade lighter than 56 interspersed with bands of white, 22, 44, 47, 11; white with dots of 21 bordered with 44. Floral swags and foliage, 6, 7, white, 43, 21, three shades lighter than 57. Scrolls, 43 outlined in 47. Background very pale cream. Theo (1).

775. PLACE DE L'OPERA saucer, 5⅝" diameter. Blank: *St. Cloud.* Backmark: S. Color code: Marli, cobalt and gold. Cavetto, flowers, 51, three shades lighter than 6, 6, 45. Theo (81).

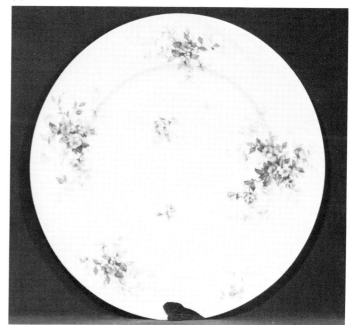

776. SALUTATION plate, 9⅝" diameter. Blank: *St. Germain.* Backmark: JJ. Color code: Flowers, 3, 4, 9, 50. Foliage, 28, 27. Shadows, 63. Theo (17).

777. NASSAU plate, 9″ diameter. Blank: *Pompadour.* Backmark: S. Color code: Cobalt and gold border. Flowers, 1, 2, 42, 12, one shade darker than 60, 54, 56, white. Foliage, 28, 29, 25, 69. Very faded gold medallion in center. Theo (40).

778. SAN FELIPE plate, 6¼″ diameter. Blank: *Plain.* Backmark: R. Color code: Flowers, 8, white, 60. Foliage, 20. Shadows, 70. Theo (81).

779. PAULINE plate, 6½″ diameter. Blank: *Plain.* Backmark: M. Color code: Flowers, 3, 5 shading to white, 59, 60, 61, white. Foliage, 5, 20, 21, 70. Theo (35).

780. PERSIA* pickle dish, 9″ by 6″. Blank: *Pilgrim.* Backmark: U. Color code: Band, 1³⁄₈″ wide, one shade lighter than 23. Flowers, 59, 60 blending with two shades lighter than 2, one shade lighter than 45; centers, 57, black. Foliage, 21, 29, black. Theo (1).

781. SUMMER FROLIC saucer, 5⁵/₈″ diameter. Blank: *Plain.* Backmark: R. Color code: Flowers, 64 with centers one shade lighter than 3. Small flowers, 3. Foliage, 19, 27 outlined in 13. Theo (56).

782. COROMANDEL* saucer, 5⁵/₈″ diameter. Blank: *Pilgrim.* Backmark: S. Color code: Band two shades darker than 42, 65, white. Marli background two shades lighter than 23. Flowers two shades lighter than 57, white, two shades darker than 42, 58, 47, white. Foliage, 22, 59, 48. Theo (56).

783. SNOWDON saucer, 5³/₈″ diameter. Blank: *Plain.* Backmark: S. Color code: Flowers, 56, white outlined in 14. Foliage, 27. Theo (17).

784. PATTERSON soup tureen lid, 9½″ diameter. Blank: *Plain.* Backmark: H. Color code: Flowers, 5, 6. Foliage two shades lighter than 28. Lattice one shade lighter than 64. Shadows, 28. Theo (1).

785. CHENONCEAUX* saucer, 5⁵/₈" diameter. Blank: *Pilgrim.* Backmark: U. Color code: Band two shades lighter than 57, white, 43, outlined in black. Marli two shades lighter than 23, edged with black line. Cartouches: Scrolls of one shade lighter than 57 containing florals of 13, 15, one shade lighter than 22. Theo (56).

786. RAJAH* cream pitcher, 4¹/₈" at widest by 2½" to lip. Blank: *Plain.* Backmark: R. Color code: Conventional border five shades lighter than 57, white, florals outlined in black; two cartouches containing birds against white background. Birds four shades darker than 60, 38, 12, and 42, 13. Flowers, 13, 60, one shade darker than 60, 38, two shades darker than 38. Theo (56).

787. CHAMBORD* plate, 6³/₈" diameter. Blank: *Pilgrim.* Backmark: R. Color code: Marli in ivory with lappett border one shade darker than 64, gold, and black. No design on inner edge of marli. Flowers, 48, touched with two shades darker than 48, 66 blending to white, 13 blending to white. Theo (1).

788. PLYMOUTH plate, 8¹/₈" diameter. Blank: *Pompadour.* Backmark: S. Color code: Flowers, 5, white, 67 touched with three shades lighter than 2, one shade darker than 53. Foliage, 28 outlined in 13. Shadows, 70. Theo (28).

789. ENCHANTMENT* plate, 7⁵/₈" diameter. Blank: *Pilgrim.*
Backmark: U. Color code: Basket two shades lighter than 57, 21, and
47, 68. Border, 23. Leaves, 21. Theo (86).

790. PAWTUCKETT plate, 6½" diameter. Blank: *Pilgrim.*
Backmark: S. Color code: Conventional border, white with black
outline against background of 65. Marli, 23. Theo (17).

791. ULSTER plate, 9¾" diameter. Blank: *Louis XV.* Backmark: JJ.
Color code: Flowers, 26, 26 touched with two shades darker than 1, 1
touched with 26. Foliage, 20, 21. Theo (35).

792. SANDIA saucer, 5½" diameter. Blank: *Plain.* Backmark: R.
Color code: Flowers, 3, 4, white, 32. Foliage, 28. Theo (12).

794. JEWEL* pitcher, 5½" to lip. Blank: *Pilgrim*. Backmark: S. Color code: Flowers five shades lighter than 57 shading to white, two shades darker than 42, 5, two shades lighter than 12. Foliage two shades darker than 21, 60 tipped with white. Theo (27).

793. ROSE MIST saucer, 5⅝" diameter. Blank: *Plain*. Backmark: R. Color code: Flowers one shade lighter than 1, eight shades lighter than 2, touched with 26. Stems and foliage, 18, four shades lighter than 22, 63. Theo (15).

795. MARTHA saucer, 5⅝" diameter. Blank: *Plain*. Backmark: U and R. Color code: Conventional border flowers, 1, three shades lighter than 2. Foliage, 27. Scrolls, 28. Theo (12).

796. CHATEAUDUN* saucer, 5⅝" diameter. Blank: *Pilgrim*. Backmark: U. Color code: Band two shades lighter than 57, 45, white outlined in black. Marli two shades lighter than 23 edged with black line. Flowers two shades lighter than 57, white, two shades darker than 42, two shades lighter than 13. Foliage, 22, white. Stems, 60. Theo (56).

797. MARIA LOUISA KENT plate, 6³/₈" diameter. Blank: *Plain.* Backmark: S. Color code: Shaped rim in gold. Flowers, 5, 10. Foliage, 26, 27, 28. Theo (89).

798. FLEMING saucer, 5½" diameter. Blank: *Louis XV.* Backmark: JJ. Color code: Flowers, 1, 2, 9. Floral shadows two shades lighter than 8 touched with 1. Foliage, 19, four shades lighter than 28, 27. Foliage shadows one shade lighter than 59. Theo (15).

799. HOLYOKE saucer, 5½" diameter. Blank: *St. Germain.* Backmark: R. Color code: Flowers, 3, 4, 5. Foliage, 29, 28, 27. Theo (47).

800. MARILY plate, 7⁵/₈" diameter. Blank: *Louis XV.* Backmark: R. Color code: Flowers, 4, 43, three shades lighter than 2, 10. Foliage two shades lighter than 22. Shadows, 34, 35. Theo (81).

801. FRANCES HARRISON HOWARD individual coffeepot, 3⁷/₈″ diameter at base, 5″ to lip. Blank: *St. Germain.* Backmark: S. Color code: Flowers, 3, 4, 42. Foliage, 20, 21. Theo (43).

802. CANDLEWICK demitasse saucer, 4⁵/₈″ diameter. Blank: *St. Germain.* Backmark: S. Color code: Flowers, 3, 2, white. Foliage, 28. Shadows two shades lighter than 34. Theo (1).

803. ETHEL plate, 9⁷/₈″ diameter. Blank: *Plain.* Backmark: U. Color code: All design, 40 and 47. Theo (1).

804. WAGON MOUND saucer, 5³/₄″ diameter. Blank: *Plain.* Backmark: R. Color code: Flowers, 5, 6. Foliage one shade darker than 27. Shadows, 67. Theo (12).

805. SALT LAKE CITY saucedish, 5″ diameter. Blank: *St. Germain.* Backmark: JJ. Color code: Flowers, 3, 4, white, 26, 25, white touched with 4. Foliage, 20, 21 touched with 4. Theo (17).

806. CELESTIAL egg cup, 2½″ tall. Blank: *Plain.* Backmark: R. Color code: Cobalt blue. Flowers and scroll, gold. Buds, white enamel. Theo (2).

807. MONTCHANIN plate, 9¾″ diameter. Blank: *Lambelle.* Backmark: S. Color code: Flowers, 63, 64, 65 touched with white. Foliage two shades darker than 27, outlined in 14. Theo (65).

808. HONEYSUCKLE saucer, 5½″ diameter. Blank: *Diana.* Backmark: Q. Color code: Flowers, 41, one shade lighter than 43. Foliage, 19, 18. Lattice, 20. Theo (15).

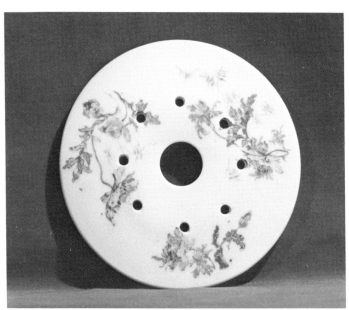

809. KELLOG butter dish insert, 4½" diameter. Blank: *Plain.* Backmark: Q. Color code: Flowers two shades lighter than 42 touched with 59, 60, 15, 25. Foliage, 25, two shades lighter than 36 touched with 15, 59 touched with 25. Theo (1).

810. WESTWOOD saucer, 5³/8" diameter. Blank: *Lambelle.* Backmark: Unknown. Color code: Flowers, 3, 4, 42. Foliage, 29, 28 touched with 4. Shadows, 34. Theo (47).

811. KINGMAN saucer, 5¼" diameter. Blank: *Plain.* Backmark: M. Color code: Conventional border with scrolls and flowers, 21, 3, four shades lighter than 2, two shades darker than 9. Theo (69).

812. MARIE* plate, 9" diameter. Blank: *Louis XV.* Backmark: JJ. Color code: Flowers, 3, white, 5, five shades lighter than 15. Foliage, 20, 28. Ribbons, 52. Note: This pattern is not the traditional arrangement of the factory-named pattern named Marie*. The flowers are more tightly packed, and there is only one spray in the cavetto. Theo (40).

316

813. GANGA* plate, 6½" diameter. Blank: *Pilgrim.* Backmark: U. Color code: Band, two shades darker than 42, white 56 outlined in black. Flowers, 47 with white, centers, 42, 22, two shades lighter than 57 white, two shades darker than 42 with two shades darker than 48. Foliage, 22, 42, 60, two shades darker than 48, 10, 5. Basket, 47, 42, 69. Theo (56).

814. WILAMETTE saucer, 5⅝" diameter. Blank: *Lambelle.* Backmark: Z. Color code: Flowers, 26, 30. Foliage, 13. Theo (15).

815. FORGET-ME-NOT oyster plate, 8³⁄₈" diameter. Blank: *Unknown.* Backmark: S. Color code: Flowers and foliage one shade deeper than 51, white, 28. Theo (3).

816. LILLE plate, 6½" diameter. Blank: *Lambelle.* Backmark: S. Color code: Flowers one shade darker than 3, white, 2, 56, 42. Foliage, 19, 20 and white, 56 touched with gold. Theo (17).

817. MONAGHAN saucer, 5″ diameter. Blank: *St. Germain.* Backmark: P. Color code: Flowers, 9, 13. Foliage, 20. Lattice, 20. Theo (47).

818. KIRKPATRICK saucer, 5½″ diameter. Blank: *Plain.* Backmark: JJ. Color code: Flowers, 1 touched with 20; 20 shading to white, two shades lighter than 53. Theo (15).

819. WINIFRED demitasse cup and saucer. Saucer, 4⅝″ diameter. Blank: *Plain.* Backmark: JJ. Color code: Flowers, 2, 3, 67, 42, 59 with white enamel. Foliage two shades lighter than 37. Theo (2).

820. SMYRNA saucer, 5½″ diameter. Blank: *Louis XV.* Backmark: S. Color code: Flowers, white, three shades lighter than 21, 59, 60. Foliage, 21. Shadows, 67. Theo (35).

821. LASSITER cup and saucer. Saucer, 5½" diameter. Blank: *Romeo*. Backmark: R. Color code: Flowers, 5, 6. Foliage, 20, 21. Theo (56).

822. EDEN* saucer, 6¼" diameter. Blank: *Pilgrim*. Backmark: R. Color code: Lappett border five shades darker than 42 with 13. Flowers two shades lighter than 57, circle white, 47 with white, five shades darker than 42 with white. Foliage, 22, two shades lighter than 22, 60, 42, two shades darker than 48. Theo (56).

823. FLORIBUNDA saucer, 5³/₈" diameter. Blank: *Plain*. Backmark: Q. Color code: Flowers, 2, 1, white, one shade lighter than 62. Foliage, 68. Theo (15).

824. FAIRYLAND cocoa cup and saucer. Saucer, 5¹/₈ diameter. Cup, 2⁷/₈" by 2³/₈". Blank: *Theo Ranson*. Backmark: S. Color code: Flowers, 6, 7, white, 5. Foliage, 27, 28. Scrolls, 32 outlined in 22. Theo (66).

825. MARY FRANCES saucer, 4¹/₂″ diameter. Blank: *Plain.* Backmark: R. Color code: Gold trim ¹/₁₆″ wide. Border one shade darker than 29, 13. Flowers, 6 touched with white, 13. Foliage 29, 48 touched with 13. Theo (1).

826. WAYNE plate, 6⁵/₈″ diameter. Blank: *Plain.* Backmark: S. Color code: Flowers, 3, 7, 42, white. Foliage, 28, 29, two shades lighter than 13. Theo (17).

827. UNNAMED saucer, 6¹/₈″ diameter. Blank: *Plain.* Backmark: R. Color code: Gold embossed. Theo (1).

828. MT. TAYLOR plate, 10″ diameter. Blank: *Plain.* Backmark: R. Color code: Flowers, 5 touched with three shades lighter than 13. Foliage, 27. Shadows two shades lighter than 10 barely touched with 5. Theo (35).

829. TRENTON platter, 14″ diameter. Blank: *Swanson**. Backmark: R. Color code: Flowers, 59, 60 shading to purple. Foliage, 28 outlined with 15, 69, 70. Theo (1).

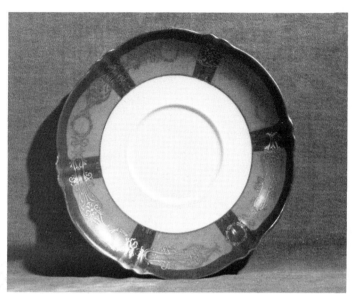

830. WINDEMERE saucer, 5³/₈″ diameter. Blank: *St. Cloud.* Backmark: AA. Color code: Conventional banded border, 22, four shades lighter than 22. Theo (15).

831. LANSING plate, 6³/₈″ diameter. Blank: *Plain.* Backmark: R. Color code: Links, gold. Flowers two shades lighter than 6, 60. Leaves, 21. Theo (1).

832. THE MOLDAU saucer, 5⁵/₈″ diameter. Blank: *Unknown.* Backmark: R. Color code: Flowers, 1, 2, white, 23 touched with 15, two shades lighter than 32. Foliage, 20, 21, 58, two shades lighter than 2. Shadows, 32. Theo (1).

833. EDGE OF THE WOODS saucer, 5⅝″ diameter. Blank: *Triple Ripple**. Backmark: U. Color code: Flowers three shades lighter and one shade darker than 6. Foliage two shades lighter than 20. Theo (81).

834. UNNAMED saucer, 5³⁄₈″ diameter. Blank: *St. Cloud.* Backmark: G. Color code: Bamboo stems and leaves, gold. Theo (12).

835. ASTER** saucer, 5⅝″ diameter. Blank: *St. Germain.* Backmark: R. Color code: Flowers, 3, white, two shades lighter than 2. Foliage, 20, 21, three shades lighter than 20. Stems, 16. Theo (1).

836. TUSCANY plate, 10″ diameter. Blank: *St. Cloud.* Backmark: S. Color code: Flowers, 11, 3, two shades darker than 42, white, 70. Foliage, 28, 29. Shadows, 58. Theo (28).

837. WEATHERSFIELD saucer, 4½″ diameter. Blank: *Romeo.* Backmark: R. Color code: Flowers, 3 shading to white. Foliage, 20 touched with three shades lighter than 22. Theo (3).

838. LAS VEGAS plate, 7⅝″ diameter. Blank: *Swanson**. Backmark: R. Color code: Flowers, 3, 4, 5, one shade darker than 9. Foliage, 29, 9 touched with 5. Shadows one shade lighter than 63, 70. Theo (54).

839. MARIE* plate, 9⅞″ diameter. Blank: *St. Germain.* Backmark: R. Color code: Bow, 63. Flowers, 5, white touched with 6. Foliage, 21 touched with 15. Theo (24).

840. BACHELOR'S BUTTONS butter insert, 4½″ diameter. Blank: *Plain.* Backmark: II. Color code: Flowers, lighter and darker shades of 62 touched with 14, 15, white. Foliage, 20 touched with 15, white. Theo (1).

841. UNNAMED cracker jar, 5½″ tall. Blank: *Rouen.* Backmark: II. Color code: White. Theo (2).

842. LAWSON saucer, 5½″ diameter. Blank: *Plain.* Backmark: R. Color code: Conventional border one shade lighter than 22, 11. Flowers, 5, white, two shades lighter than 42. Foliage, 28, 27. Theo (40).

843. WHITE CLAY CREEK saucer, 5³/8″ diameter. Blank: *Geisha.* Backmark: R. Color code: Flowers, 3 touched with 4. Small flowers two shades lighter than 3. Foliage, 20, 21. Ferns, 59. Theo (35).

844. VALHALLA demitasse saucer, 4⁵/8″ diameter. Blank: *Swanson*.* Backmark: S. Color code: Conventional border, cobalt with elaborate gold trim. Theo (1).

324

845. LUCILLE* saucer, 4⁵⁄₈″ diameter. Blank: *Plain.* Backmark: R. Color code: Flowers, 5, 16, white. Shadow, 68, 5. Foliage, 21 touched with 16. Shadow, 68. Lattice, 21 outlined in 16. Theo (1).

846. BRISTOL plate, 9⁵⁄₈″ diameter. Blank: *Romeo.* Backmark: R. Color code: Flowers, 1, 2, 42, 70, white. Foliage, 22, 24 tipped with 2. Shadows, 70. Theo (12).

847. TUCSON plate, 6³⁄₈″ diameter. Blank: *Ruby.* Backmark: JJ. Color code: Flowers, 4 shading to white. Foliage, 20 touched with two shades lighter than 22. Theo (7).

848. LEICESTER saucer, 5³⁄₈″ diameter. Blank: *Louis XV.* Backmark: JJ. Color code: Flowers, 1, 2, 56. Foliage, 21, 20. Ribbon, 56. Theo (17).

849. DESDEMONA plate, 7½" diameter. Blank: *Plain.* Backmark: R. Color code: Conventional border two shades lighter than 40 outlined in two shades lighter than 13. Flowers, 4, 5, white. Theo (15).

850. FIRENZE saucer, 6" diameter. Blank: *St. Germain.* Backmark: S. Color code: Scrolls and gold with 22. Theo (56).

851. MAYPOLE saucer, 5⅝" diameter. Blank: *Plain.* Backmark: S. Color code: Conventional border, 45, 13, five shades darker than 66. Flowers, 5, 8, 53. Foliage, 20. Note: This also comes without the inner black line. Theo (12).

852. GARRIOTT saucer, 5½" diameter. Blank: *Parabere.* Backmark: II. Color code: Flowers, 5, 6, 20. Foliage, 21, 20, white. Shadows, 34, 23. Theo (12).

853. UNNAMED cup and saucer. Saucer, 5³/₈" diameter. Blank: *St. Cloud.* Backmark: AA. Color code: Gold trim. Theo (2).

854. HAZEL butter dish insert, 4⁵/₁₆" diameter. Blank: *Plain.* Backmark: Q. Color code: Flowers, 23 touched with 69 and 14. Foliage, 6 touched with 14. Scroll, 69 touched with 23, 14. Theo (1).

855. LIZA ANNE saucedish, 5" diameter. Blank: *Plain.* Backmark: M. Color code: Flowers, 5, white, 7. Foliage one shade lighter than 28. Shadows, 59. Theo (17).

856. WILLARD cup, 3½" diameter. Blank: *Louis XV.* Backmark: M. Color code: Flowers, 3, 4, 8 touched with five shades lighter than 2. Foliage, 27, 28. Shadows, 8, 3, 56. Theo (40).

857. CADOT saucer, 4⁵/₈" diameter. Blank: *Caroline.* Backmark: JJ. Color code: Flowers, 3, 2, 42, white. Foliage one shade lighter than 28. Shadows four shades lighter than 20. Theo (1).

859. THE VARENNES* platter, 12" by 8¼". Blank: *St. Germain.* Backmark: G. Color code: Flowers two shades lighter than 45, 3. Foliage, 20. Stems, 15. Note: This platter is shown to demonstrate the change in appearance of the same pattern when on a different blank and to show also the distribution of design on a larger piece. Theo (72).

858. LIANCOURT butter pat, 3" diameter. Blank: *Wavelets**. Backmark: R. Color code: Flowers, 3, 4, 64. Foliage, 27. Bows, 60. Theo (78).

860. BRADFORD plate, 9⁵/₈" diameter. Blank: *Wavelets**. Backmark: S. Color code: Flowers three shades lighter than 2, white, 3, 5. Foliage, 21, one shade darker than 18. Theo (54).

328

861. UNNAMED cocoa pot, 8″ to lip. Blank: *Caroline*. Backmark: S. Color code: White. Note unusual employment of blank on a serving piece. Theo (1).

862. UNNAMED plate, 6³/₈″ diameter. Blank: *St. Germain*. Backmark: R. Color code: Gold trim. Theo (4).

863. AFTERNOON SHADOWS saucer, 5½″ diameter. Blank: *Plain*. Backmark: S. Color code: Flowers, 8, 6, white. Foliage two shades lighter than 21. Shadows three shades lighter than 53. Theo (12).

864. ARCHER saucer, 5¾″ diameter. Blank: *St. Raphael*. Backmark: JJ. Color code: Orchids, 63 touched with 3, 2, 21. Carnations, 65, white touched with 2; 6 touched with 2 and white. Forget-me-nots, 6, 5 white touched with 2. Morning-glories, 6, 5, white touched with 2. Flowers, 63 touched with 3, 2, 21; 6 touched with 2, touched with white. Foliage, 21, white touched with 2. Theo (1).

865. ST. LAWRENCE saucer, 5″ diameter. Blank: *Romeo.* Backmark: R. Color code: Flowers two shades lighter than 1 and white. Foliage, 19. Scrolls, 56. Stems four shades lighter than 3. Theo (31).

866. ANTOINETTE ramekin, 3¹/₈″ diameter. Blank: *Triple Ripple**. Backmark: S. Color code: Flowers, 1, two shades lighter than 2, 42, 9. Foliage, 28, 30, 18. Theo (43).

867. STOWE plate, 6½″ diameter. Blank: *Triple Ripple**. Backmark: R. Color code: Flowers and foliage, 1, white, 56, 42, 21, 20. Theo. (17).

868. RUTH saucer, 5³/₈″ diameter. Blank: *Pilgrim.* Backmark: U. Color code: Conventional border three shades darker than 42 with 13. Foliage, 20. Flowers, 64, 65, two shades darker than 9, 23. Theo. (12).

869. SPRINGMAID plate, 7½" diameter. Blank: *Plain.* Backmark: R. Color code: Conventional border two shades lighter than 12, 20, two shades darker than 20. Theo. (12).

870. ABILENE plate, 6¼" diameter. Blank: *Marie Antoinette.* Backmark: S. Color code: Flowers, 61, 42, 3 touched with three shades lighter than 2, white outlined in three shades lighter than 2. Stems two shades lighter than 13. Shadows, 70. Theo (12).

871. MEMPHIS saucer, 5⅝" diameter. Blank: *Plain.* Backmark: S. Color code: Flowers, 1, 8, 59, white. Foliage, 27, five shades lighter than 15. Shadows, 59. Theo (40).

872. SCYLLA saucer, 8⅞" diameter. Blank: *Louis XV.* Backmark: P. Color code: Flowers one shade lighter than 1 shading to white, three shades darker than 62, 52. Foliage two shades lighter than 19. Shadows, 70. Theo (15).

873. CLOVELLY egg cup, 1³/₄″ diameter, by 2³/₈″ tall. Blank: *Plain.* Backmark: R. Color code: Flowers, 1, three shades darker than 1. Foliage, 22. Shadows two shades darker than 34. Theo (56).

874. MARCIA dinner plate, 9³/₄″ diameter. Blank: *Rouen.* Backmark: Q. Color code: Border design one shade darker than 36; gold design on rim and center. Theo (65).

875. SALMANCA butter pat, 3″ diameter. Blank: *Lambelle.* Backmark: R. Color code: Rim, gold on design and bows. Flowers, 29, 30 touched with white and 15, touched wtih 15, 29, and white. Foliage two shades lighter than 15 touched with 15 and white. Shadow foliage, 32. Theo (1).

876. ANDERSON saucer, 5³/₄″ diameter. Blank: *Aigle.* Backmark: R. Color code: Flowers, 3, 4, white. Folige, 21, 22 touched with 7. Theo (12).

877. THE ARDENNES* saucer, 6¼" diameter. Blank: *Romeo.*
Backmark: S. Color code: Flowers, 4, 3, white. Foliage, 20, 21,
white, 13. Stems, 13. Shadows, 59, 70. Theo (56).

878. SELDON saucer, 5" diameter. Blank: *Plain.* Backmark: R.
Color code: Band chain design three shades darker than 42, black,
white. Scroll two shades darker than 65 outlined in black. Flowers, 2,
6, touched with white. Foliage one shade darker than 21. Theo (1).

879. GWENDOLYN soup bowl, 7³/₈" diameter. Blank: *Louis XV.*
Backmark: S. Color code: Flowers, 3, 4, 42, 61 touched with three
shades lighter than 2, two shades lighter than 2. Shadows, 68. Theo
(40).

880. SEDGLEY saucer, 5¹/₈" diameter. Blank: *Theo. Ranson.*
Backmark: Q. Color code: Flowers, 56 touched with 2; 42 touched
with 2 and one shade darker than 63; 5 touched with 2 and white.
Shadow, 32. Theo (1).

881. ALEXANDRIA plate, 9¾″ diameter. Blank: *Feston-Chene.* Backmark: S. Color code: Flowers, 59. Wreath, 5, 6. Foliage, 21. Theo (65).

882. GALWAY demitasse cup and saucer. Saucer, 4⅝″ diameter. Blank: *Theo Ranson.* Backmark: S. Color code: Flowers, 38, with white, 9, touches of 14, 34. Foliage, 21. Theo (56).

883. ALANNA cup, 3¼″ diameter. Blank: *Triple Ripple*.* Backmark: JJ. Color code: Flowers, 4, 5 touched with two shades lighter than 2. Foliage, 27, 28. Theo (23).

884. SWEET RUE saucer, 5⅝″ diameter. Blank: *St. Germain.* Backmark: R. Color code: Flowers one shade darker than 5. Foliage, 18 tipped with 21. Theo (15).

334

885. AFTERGLOW plate, 6³/₈" diameter. Blank: *Louis XV.*
Backmark: R. Color code: Flowers, 1, 3, white, 42, touched with 13.
Foliage, 27, 28. Shadows, 27. Theo (15).

886. GRAND BALLROOM saucer, 6¼" diameter. Blank: *Geisha.*
Backmark: JJ. Color code: Flowers, 5 shading nearly to white touched
with three shades lighter than 2. Swags, 28, 30. Theo (15).

887. HARFLEUR plate, 8⁵/₈" diameter. Blank: *Louis XV.* Backmark:
S. Color code: Flowers four shades darker than 62, 60, 58. Foliage two
shades lighter than 28, white, touches of 62. Shadows two shades
lighter than 36. Theo (56).

888. LISBONNE saucer, 5⁵/₈" diameter. Blank: *St. Germain.*
Backmark: R. Color code: Flowers, 1, 50, 70. Ribbon, 20. Foliage,
20, 21, 16. Theo (1).

889. VERNA LEE saucer, 5½″ diameter. Blank: *St. Germain.* Backmark: Q. Color code: Flowers, 61, 62 touched with white. Foliage two shades lighter than 20. Shadows, 32. Ribbon, 65. Theo (1).

890. KEMPER plate, 9¾″ diameter. Blank: *Embossed* St. Cloud.* Backmark: M. Color code: Flowers, 3, 4, three shades lighter than 2. Foliage, 26, 22 touched with three shades lighter than 2. Theo (37).

891. CARLISLE PLACE saucer, 5⅝″ diameter. Blank: *Louis XV.* Backmark: S. Color code: Flowers, 61, white, 51. Foliage, 26. Theo (35).

892. DENISE saucer, 5⅝″ diameter. Blank: *Diamond.* Backmark: S. Color code: Flowers, 1, white, 3, two shades lighter than 53. Foliage, 28. Shadows, 69. Theo (47).

894. AQUITAINIA* plate, 9½". Blank: *Unknown.* Backmark: U and S. Color code: Rim ¹/₁₆" gold. Band background two shades lighter than 23. Rim flowers, shades of 2 touched with white; shades of 57 touched with white. Centers one shade lighter than 45, 13. Nasturtiums, 13, 45, 21. Rim foliage, 21 touched with 45. Inner rim two shades darker than 57 with one shade darker than 45. Bowl in center, 65 touched with white. Flowers, shades of 2 touched with white; shades of 57 touched with white; 45 touched with 13. Foliage, 21. Theo (1).

893. L'ETE plate, 9⁵/₈" diameter. Blank: *Marie Antoinette.* Backmark: T. Color code: Flowers one shade lighter than 62, 23. Foliage three shades lighter than 34. Theo (1).

895. EUBANK saucer, 4¾" diameter. Blank: *Pilgrim.* Backmark: U. Color code: Conventional border, gold rim, gold bars on marli outlined in black. Scrolls, 42 outlined in black. Flowers, 5, 2, both outlined in black. Foliage, two shades lighter than 36. Theo (1).

896. CECILY soup tureen lid, 9½" diameter. Blank: *Lambelle.* Backmark: S. Color code: Flowers one and two shades darker than 1; 63 touched with two shades darker than 1, 67, two shades darker than 9. Foliage, 20, 21. Theo (1).

897. DARIEN saucer, 5½" diameter. Blank: *Pilgrim.* Backmark: U. Color code: Conventional border background, black. Flowers, 3, 4, three shades lighter than 57. Foliage, 20. Cartouches edged in 20; flowers two shades darker than 4, shading to white against background one shade lighter than 45. Flowers, 43, 3, 4, 5. Foliage, 20. Background, cream. Theo (12).

898. MC CAULEY plate, 6½" diameter. Blank: *Marie Antoinette.* Backmark: R. Color code: Flowers, 6 shading to white. Foliage, 20 outlined with 2. Shadow one shade lighter than 58. Scroll, 20 outlined with 2. Theo (1).

899. LITTLETON plate, 8¾" diameter. Blank: *Plain.* Backmark: S. Color code: Flowers one shade lighter than 1, white, two shades lighter than 9, 3, five shades lighter than 2. Folige, 28, white touched with four shades lighter than 15. Theo (12).

900. ARBUTUS saucer, 5½" diameter. Blank: *Plain.* Backmark: R. Color code: Flowers, 64, 3. Foliage, 20, and one and two shades darker. Theo (15).

901. MARIKO-SAN saucer, 5³/₈″ diameter. Blank: *Chippendale.* Backmark: S. Color code: Border one shade darker than 65, two shades darker than 42, white, on iridescent ivory. Vase three shades darker than 66. Flowers three shades darker than 66, 42, 47. Foliage two shades darker than 21. Theo (81).

902. EDWARD cup and saucer. Saucer, 4⁵/₈″ diameter. Blank: *Swanson.* Backmark: S. Color code: Cobalt and gold. Theo (1).

903. SPRING GROVE saucer, 4¹/₈″ diameter. Blank: *Wavelets*.* Backmark: II. Color code: Flowers, 1, 2, 25, 56, one shade darker than 60, two shades lighter than 12. Foliage two shades lighter than 22. Theo (1).

904. PETERSBOROUGH plate, 6⁵/₈″ diameter. Blank: *Louis XV.* Backmark: KK. Color code: Flowers, 3, 4, 32, white, 42, 2 shades lighter than 13. Foliage, 29. Shadow, 63. Theo (17).

339

905. EUYRELEE* saucer, 5³/₈" diameter. Blank: *Plain.* Backmark: V. Color code: Conventional border, 13 and four shades lighter than 57. Cream background with three cartouches in cavetto. Two horns of plenty in three shades lighter than 57 and 13 in fan of same color. Flowers one shade lighter than 3. Small flowers five shades lighter than 57. Centers in three shades lighter than 13, also 3. Foliage, 22 and two shades lighter than 22. Theo (15).

906. SARALEE plate, 8½" diameter. Blank: *St. Cloud.* Backmark: JJ. Color code: Flowers, 1, white edged in three shades lighter than 13. Foliage, 19. Shadows, 32. Theo (17).

907. TIPTON plate, 7½" diameter. Blank: *Louis XV.* Backmark: R. Color code: Flowers, 2, 3, touched with white, 24. Centers white touched with 2, 24, 32, touched with 2, 24, white. Foliage, 32 touched with white, two shades darker than 21, touched with 24, 2, white. Theo (1).

908. WHEELWRIGHT plate, 8⁵/₈" diameter. Blank: *St. Germain.* Backmark: R. Color code: Flowers, white, 1, two shades lighter than 2. Foliage, 20, two shades lighter than 20. Shadows, 67. Theo (1).

909. SANTORINI saucer, 5½″ diameter. Blank: *Plain.* Backmark: Q. Color code: Flowers and foliage, 20, 21, 24, 32, 59, two shades darker than 60. Theo (1).

910. SUMMERHILL saucer, 5½″ diameter. Blank: *St. Cloud.* Backmark: R. Color code: Flowers, 9, 19, 17. Foliage, 9, 19, 17. Theo (47).

911. STONE MOUNTAIN saucer, 5³/₈″ diameter. Blank: *Louis XV.* Backmark: S. Color code: Flowers, 25, two shades darker than 25, white outlined in 13, two shades lighter than 32. Theo (17).

912. MORRIS DANCERS saucer, 5½″ diameter. Blank: *Juliet.* Backmark: S. Color code: Border two shades lighter than 22 with white dots, gold trim. Flowers, 1, 2, 3, 61. Foliage, 21, 22 outlined with 2. Theo (1).

913. EDNA saucer, 5³/₈″ diameter. Blank: *Plain.* Backmark: S. Color code: Scrolls, 9, white, outlined in two shades lighter than 14. Flowers, 56 touched with 14. Foliage, 32, 63. Theo (1).

Index